ENERGY SECRETS OF GLASTONBURY TOR

Energy Secrets
of
Glastonbury Tor

Nicholas R. Mann

Green Magic

The photographs and pictures in this book
are by the author unless otherwise stated

This edition is published by
Green Magic
The Long Barn
Sutton Mallet
Somerset
TA7 9AR

Typeset by Academic + Technical, Bristol
Printed and bound by Antony Rowe Ltd.

Cover image by Nicholas R. Mann

Cover design by Chris Render

Cover production by Tania Lambert

ISBN 0 9542 9635 4

Reprinted 2005

GREEN MAGIC

CONTENTS

INTRODUCTION

Ten thousand years ago, as people stood on the edge of the broad vale that was to become the Summerland, the Somerset Levels, and looked at the dramatic hill in its centre, they knew what it was. They understood the significance it held as they felt its presence, its power and its compelling pull on their minds, hearts and imaginations. They began to leave their mark upon the hill as they sculpted it closer and closer to the ideal appropriate for such a place. They, and the subsequent generations that dwelt in the area, understood the hill perfectly: It was a natural temple, a cosmic axis, a world mountain and a gateway between the worlds.

For them, the island with the Tor at its centre had extraordinary energetic qualities. It was a place of power, not to be idly visited. It was an earthly paradise where this power was focused and increased, and where communication was made between the worlds. It was the place of transition for the soul, and they knew how to contact and work with this exchange. Their hearts, minds and bodies were attuned to the elements, to nature and the stars, and they knew the times of inflow and outflow, of the systole and diastole of life, death and creation. The Tor gave them an altar, a fulcrum, a point of leverage within the cosmos, where they could gather at appropriate times to harmonise with and influence the subtle but powerful forces of life.

When I saw the Tor for the first time, I sensed this power. And the longer I lived here and the more I learnt about the mysteries of Avalon the more I realised that a practice was maintained here that spanned thousands of years. This practice was concerned with the knowledge of soul transformation and transition and, at times, a school, an Order, flourished upon the island to teach these mysteries and carry out its tasks. The original rule of the Order of Avalon was to build nothing upon the island, to do no harm to the wild nature of the place, including the sacred herds and flocks of animals, and so preserve and enhance the natural law and primordial harmony that facilitated the journey of the soul.

I learnt about all this because it was in existence when the first chroniclers came to the island. They encountered the traditions and practices of the Order of Avalon, recorded, and continued them in their own way. For the Christians, the island became the place where the Son of God walked and where the first (and subsequently the greatest) church dedicated to the Mother of God was built from nothing but the mud and reeds of the marshes. The tradition developed among mythographers and historians and Avalon became the place where the sword of the sovereignty of the land, Excalibur, was forged and then returned to its maker. It became the place where its greatest king, Arthur, beheld the vision that led to his victories and it was where he returned, when mortally wounded, to cross over to the other side. It became the place where the font of life itself in the form of the Holy Grail was buried and with it, the transforming blood of the alchemists. Eventually, just to be buried in the soil of the Abbey cemetery, the 'holyeste erthe' of all Christendom, meant salvation; and many are the seekers who still come to Avalon to discover the extraordinary treasure buried in the earth here.

Today, many who come to Avalon share the same appreciation and awareness of the power of the place as those people in the past. Avalon, with the Tor at its heart, still opens itself for those who open themselves to it. Many I have spoken to, on hearing the ideas expressed in this book, say that it puts into words what they already know – what they felt when they saw the Tor for the first time. I do not take this as a criticism for my lack of originality but as verification of what I have written. I have tried to put into words appropriate for our times the long-standing knowledge of the Tor as a soul portal – a powerful vortex of natural and spiritual power that can transform lives. I invite you to enter this book, to see if the message contained within resonates with your understanding of the Isle of Avalon.

* * *

Please note the book proceeds in three sections. The first section sketches out the energy of the Tor and its nature as the gateway between the worlds. The second section fills out the details of the history, geography and traditions of the Tor. The final section builds upon this base to provide a description of the energy of the Tor and the function of the

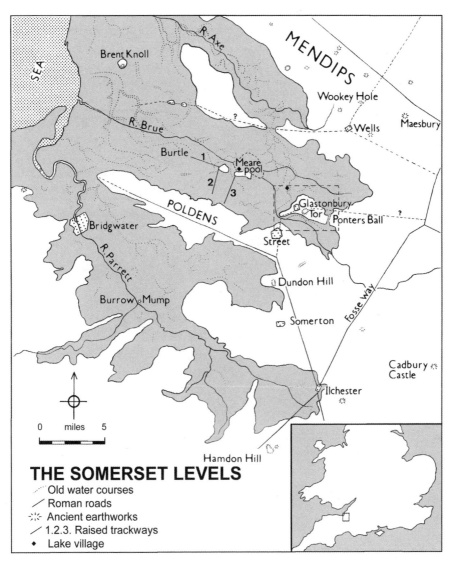

▲ **The Somerset Levels.** This map locates Glastonbury in Britain and shows its relationship to the area of the former 'inland sea.' Although peat marshland and raised bog conditions predominated by 4000 BCE, people were attracted to the rich natural resources of the area. They built ritual monuments, they constructed wooden trackways over the marsh, their ships found passage along the waterways and eventually lake villages, hill forts and trading ports flourished. The Somerset Levels formed a neutral zone on the borders of the surrounding Celtic tribes. The Romans began the first serious drainage of the Levels and as large areas are only a few feet above sea level, drainage continues to this day.

3

soul portal. The boxes spread throughout the book provide additional information, which although relevant to their location in the text can be read separately. Finally, please note that CE, the 'Common Era' and BCE, 'Before the Common Era' replace AD and BC respectively.

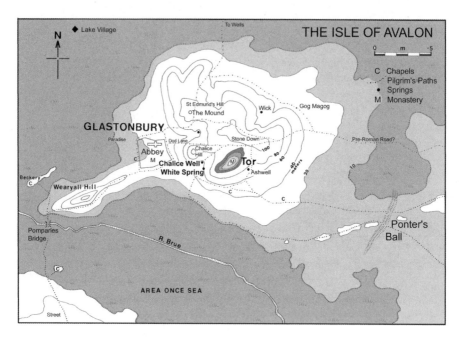

▲ **The Isle of Avalon.** Once known as *Ynis Witrin*, the 'Isle of Glass', the island consists of three hills dominated by the Tor, while a fourth hill forms a limb out to the southwest. Once surrounded by waterways and difficult marshland, a narrow strip of land made the only dry connection with the mainland to the east. This entranceway was cut across by a massive ditch and bank known as Ponter's Ball; this effectively ringed the island with water. The pattern of roads is largely determined by pilgrim's paths running to and from Glastonbury Abbey; although at least one, Dod Lane, running due east–west, is pre-Roman.

PART ONE

IMAGINING THE UNIMAGINABLE: DEFINING THE DYNAMIC OF THE TOR

THE NATIONAL TRUST VISIT ATLANTIS

In 2002 the National Trust, who own Glastonbury Tor, placed new signs on the recently improved approaches. The signs say 'the tor has been a place of pilgrimage for over 10,000 years'. I was excited by this claim, as I have never found any firm evidence to prove that people with spiritual intentions were here at this early time. Had the NT found something new? No, alas, they had not. Inquiries revealed they meant to say that there was evidence for people first being present in the area about then, but they didn't actually have any proof that the people's reasons for being there were for pilgrimage. I was disappointed; doubly so as the new signs, unlike the old, said nothing about the Tor being the castle of the King of Fairy. The National Trust play it safe once again, I thought; but somehow, inadvertently, they were entirely right. Ten thousand years ago visitors did conduct journeys for spiritual purposes to the Tor.

What someone in a National Trust office was imagining, but couldn't for obvious reasons come right out and say, was that the visitors to the Tor came from Atlantis, a land now under the sea. Ten thousand years ago there was still a land bridge between Britain and the Continent, and the memory of the land below the waves is preserved in the Atlantean mythic tradition. The mythology says that the Atlanteans came to the Tor because the sea destroyed their temples, but here in the bleak north-eastern remnant of their land a natural temple remained. This temple was capable of carrying out some of the work performed by their now destroyed temple pyramids. The temples of Atlantis had many purposes, most of which are unknown to the NT, but the one important function of soul conveyance could be carried out on the Tor.[1]

Put at its simplest, the task was to gather up the host of incoming and outgoing souls and guide them to their respective destinations. The Tor as a beacon on the borders of life and death guided and assisted the soul on its transformational journey between the worlds. The Atlanteans, it is said, had the need for just such a beacon, and they understood the Tor functioned in this manner.

The Tor needed some reshaping to enhance its role and this was swiftly carried out. The engineers were assisted in their work by the lack of trees due to the coldness of the climate and by the natural terracing of the Tor. It was a matter of connecting the naturally formed ledges of the Tor so they formed continuous terraces upon its flanks. Seven main

7

terraces were required, and these were fashioned in a short space of time. Once accomplished, the seven terraces resonated with and enhanced the subtle fields of a vortex of energy created by an unusual aquifer – a water bearing system – within the Tor.

Although the Atlantean story is little more than that, a story, my research into the Tor – and indeed into all the Avalonian stories – uncovers exactly what the story describes. The aquifer within the Tor, created many millions of years ago by natural forces and maintained today by rainwater, has energetic properties that are suited to certain tasks. The sandstone, clay, marlstone and limestone layers that form the Tor and which contain the water of the aquifer are saturated with calcium and iron. One spring of the Tor – the White Spring – taps the top of the aquifer; another spring – the Red or Blood Spring – taps the bottom. This unusual two-layer geophysical system causes the atomic and ionic bonds of the elements dissolved in the water within it to hold a polarity of electromagnetic forces in a flux capable of interacting with and influencing the subtle energies of the human psychophysical system.

In recent years, dowsers have investigated the Tor and called the negatively and positively charged currents of energy they have found there the 'Michael and Mary lines'.[2] These energies move and are formed across the country, but in this specific location they form a force field capable of appearing to and assisting the soul in the transitional realm between the worlds. In essence, the Tor contains a dynamic emergent energy field that when intentionally enhanced appears in a form that is sensed by and is familiar to the soul. The conditional life experiences of the soul affect perception, but beyond the physical senses the soul is free to perceive on other frequencies and it generally experiences these frequencies or energy fields in a unified or a non-localised manner. Matter is no longer seen as a collection of distinct objects separate in time and space, but in its true form as interacting and interdependent energy creating time and space. The discarnate soul 'sees' the Tor as an unfolding swirling vortex of dragon or serpent-like forms made up of multiple colours moving through mists, that build into shining, spherical, vesical, crystalline or dome-like formations with an internal structure resembling an opening, a tunnel or a door.

I learnt from my research that the people who understood this extra-ordinary dynamic of the Tor – and established a school here, whether or not they were from the time of Atlantis – worked to enhance these energy fields on a regular basis. They enhanced the fundamental energy field created by the aquifer in the Tor through visualisation, toning, prayer

▲ Aerial view of the Tor. Photograph by Kevin Redpath.

and other activities. They 'co-operated with the force of intelligence on the other side' – as one dowser put it – to achieve the desired effect. Once operating strongly, the mutually generated energies of the Tor vortex were perceived over a wide area, allowing many souls to pass through its portal to different realms. Apparently the formations would collapse from time to time, sending energy out for the revitalising of other realms such as that of the plants and trees, and then time was needed for the restoration of the full functioning of the portal. I also learnt from my sources that the two main control devices for the energy fields were the Red and the White Springs. These, like the negative and positive terminals of a battery or a capacitor, could influence the operating frequencies and so affect the functioning of the system as a whole.

THE TOR: A GLOBAL POWER CENTRE

The Tor is a powerful focus and conduit for the movement of universal energy and all who view the Tor on a journey to the Isle of Avalon consciously or unconsciously comprehend its remarkable dynamic. Those writers who were consciously aware of the properties of the Tor did not hesitate to describe them in terms of extraordinarily powerful

▲ **The Terraces on the Tor.** The terraces on the Tor are formed by a combination of natural and human actions. The Tor and the terraces assumed their basic shape due to geological action and then developed through several periods of human intervention. The first period of intervention began in prehistory when the goal was to enhance the Tor as the *axis mundi* – the world centre. The second period was during the time of the Abbey (and the monastery of St. Michael's upon the Tor) when it was necessary to cultivate high and dry land and it was felt the creation of a seven-tiered Calvary Mount could only add to the holy atmosphere of the isle. The third period was the continuation of the use of the terraces as agricultural lynchets after the closing of the Abbey up to the nineteenth century. The final period is today as people thread the path formed by the terraces of an enormous multi-dimensional labyrinth.

global and cosmic energies. The occultist Dion Fortune, for example, describes the Tor as a 'strange hill, and round it winds a spiral way in three great coils ... such mounts as this were always sacred to the sun'.[3] The psychometrist Iris Campbell said that 'Glastonbury Tor is raised over an epicentre of magnetism, and that which is located there is continually churning up underneath'.[4] The writer and founder of the Silent Minute, Wellesley Tudor Pole, saw many beings around the Tor – ancient magicians, Devas, dragons, light workers, guides and Angelic hierarchies – each working a part of the strongly vibrating 'auric sheafs' of power (see Appendix 3). In every case the descriptions make it clear that the Tor consists of complex, winding vortices of energy turning around a pronounced vertical axis. The Tor is indeed a world axis – the *axis mundi* – on a scale to connect earth and sky. It is a bridge between the above and the below, between the terrestrial and extra-terrestrial. It is the bridge between the inner and the outer, the seen and the unseen dimensions of the universe.

The world axis is represented in all spiritual traditions by a mountain, a hill, a column, or by some other high and holy feature. It is said to be the centre of the world. The traditions say that at the core of the world axis is an opening through which it is possible to journey to the worlds above and the worlds below. Traditional knowledge also says that Polaris is attached to the summit of the world axis, and, as all the stars turn around the pole star, so all the worlds turn around it.[5] The 158 metre high Tor provides a classic example of the world mountain lying in the centre of its sea level plain. The plain gives the Tor focus, height and depth, while – as described in the section on the Glastonbury Zodiac – the cosmos is constellated upon its surface in the form of the astrological zodiac.

There are many legends attached to Glastonbury, but all repeat in one way or another that Avalon is the transitional place where the soul comes and goes through the opening in the Tor. The Tor, as *axis mundi*, the world centre, has an opening within it. Avalon, the legends say, is an earthly paradise, the memory of which is preserved in local place names: 'Paradise Lane' on Stone Down, and 'Paradise' in the area where the town meets the marshes. Upon this 'Isle of Apples, truly fortunate,' runs Camden's translation of an ancient ode, 'the fields require no rustic hand, but Nature only cultivates the land.' Tennyson picked up the otherworldly theme: 'The island valley of Avilion, where falls not hail, or rain, or any snow...'[6] And then there is the Fairy King himself, Gwynn ap Nudd, who rides out with the Wild Hunt to bring the souls of the recently deceased through the doorway on the Tor into the Otherworld.

Those visitors who appreciate the greater synchronicities between the landscape and the body – and especially the fact that two springs, one red, one white, are present here – go even further, and impute to the Tor qualities specific to vital centres or systems in the body. Dion Fortune did just this, and called it 'Avalon of the Heart'. Others say it is a crown chakra, a solar plexus chakra, and a point of vital importance on the meridians of the global energy body. The Christian legends bring the blood and water from Christ's body to the Isle and much ink has been spilt over the Grail and Blood Mysteries of Avalon. A more recent informant, described in Appendix 2, said Avalon is about the DNA: 'It carries the universal energy dynamic encoded in the genes.' Given the vortices of energy created by the aquifer within the Tor, what part does the Tor play in the relationship between the human body and the body of the earth? Why is it this, and what makes the Tor a natural global power centre?

I describe in this book how the springs, aquifer and axes of the Tor generate and are generated by a vortical energy field to form a power centre of terrestrial and cosmic proportions. The Tor is a point upon the global body of the earth where universal energies, variously described as *Ch'i*, *mana*, *Ki*, *prana*, *orgone*, *yin* and *yang*, meet, and through their alignment with the energy of the soul perform vital transitional functions. The Tor is a point upon the surface of the earth where the energy meridians of the universe harmonise with the intentions of those working for the well being of all life, and is specifically a place where beneficial influence is effected upon the transformational journey of the soul.

ENDNOTES

1. For the Atlantean stories of the Tor see Wellesley Tudor Pole, 1968, pp. 97–104 or look up Atlantis in the work of Dion Fortune.

2. Hamish Miller and Paul Broadhurst in their 1995 publication *The Sun and the Serpent*.

3. *Avalon of the Heart*, Dion Fortune, 1934. For Tudor Pole, see for example Sandys & Lehmann *The Awakening Letters*, 1965, pp. 69–80.

4. Iris Campbell is recorded in the works of J. Foster Forbes, here, *Giants, Myths and Megaliths*, 1945.

5. Mircea Eliade, 1958 cf. world mountain references.

6. Camden quoted from G. Wright 1870, p. 20. Tennyson, *Arthurian Idylls*.

PART TWO

ANCIENT AVALON: SOURCES AND RESOURCES

CHALICE WELL

A complex subterranean system provides the water of the Red or Blood Spring that rises at the Chalice Well. The water, people say, may originate from the locality, from the Mendip Hills, or from further away. It may even be juvenile water, that is, water from deep within the earth emerging to the surface for the first time. No one is sure. Generally, I have found the more mystical the informant the more distant the source of water, while more pragmatic people, such as hydrologists, think the source is much closer to hand. In this section, I examine the evidence for the source of the water and this begins with the fact that a spring with a high iron (chalybeate) content rises at Chalice Well. This mineralisation, plus the reported constant rate of flow of 25,000 gallons

▲ Chalice Well lid

15

(110,000 litres) per day, plus the constant temperature of 52 °F (11 °C), suggest a distant origin, as the deeper and more distant the source the more likely the water is to be mineralised, constant and unaffected by seasonal rainfall.

Tradition says that the spring broke out of the ground when Joseph of Arimathea buried the cup used by Christ at the last supper below Chalice Hill. 'This spring, however, was not of ordinary water', wrote George Wright in 1870 quoting typical local beliefs, 'it was the veritable "water of life", leaving in its track its signs in blood . . .'[1]

The present keepers of the spring are the Chalice Well Trust. The Trust was founded in 1958, and before the gardens were laid out the Trust sponsored archaeological excavations. The Trust had received reports from dowsers that early Christian graves and a chapel were on the site and finding evidence of this would validate popular Glastonbury traditions. The excavations began in 1960 under the competent direction of Philip Rahtz who, again sponsored by Chalice Well Trust, was to later excavate the Tor. At this time a school occupied the site and the restoration process included removing the forbidding four-storey building that stood at the bottom of the gardens. The Trust were to be disappointed as the excavations yielded surprisingly little evidence of early occupation, but it was learnt that the yew trees, which are present throughout the garden, had always been there. A stump of yew over three metres underground yielded a radiocarbon date of around 300 CE. Rahtz found that the valley floor had risen considerably over the years, and he wondered whether the challenges this presented and the small area examined due to the buildings on the site were responsible for the small amount of evidence obtained.

In Celtic, Classical and in subsequent traditions, the yew tree is associated with death and rebirth. It is possible for a yew to reach extreme old age – they have the greatest longevity of any European tree – to achieve a massive girth, to become hollow, and, when the time is right, to either send new shoots upward from the centre of the tree or for new seeds to grow in the hollow remains of the old. Yew berries are red and toxic, and it is the tradition to plant a yew tree in Church graveyards where it is said 'to send a root to the mouth of every corpse'. Assuming that yew trees were always present around the Blood Spring – and the evidence of the stump indicates they were – then it is possible that the affinities between the trees and the red waters of the spring were not just noted but also deliberately cultivated. The water of the red spring originally flowed from out of a grove of yew trees in a stream that covered everything it touched with a vivid blood red.

A further attribution to the Chalice Well concerns the well shaft and the unusual polygonal chamber beside it. It is said the chamber, which can be rapidly drained and filled, was used for Druidic initiation rituals that involved drowning followed by resuscitation. This idea probably arose after claims were made that the stonework of both the well shaft and the lower courses of the polygonal chamber were pre-Roman. Although the sides of the well shaft are built from large blocks of stone without mortar – a style of construction that is early – both Rahtz and Dr. Raleigh Radford (who worked on the Abbey) thought that the well shaft was built around 1200 CE. It used stones recycled from the Abbey Church that had burnt down in 1184. They also thought that the polygonal brick-roofed chamber dated to the 18th century. It was an addition made to the well when Glastonbury became popular as a spa and a reservoir was needed to create the pressure to carry the water into town. It is hazardous to suggest so ancient a time as the Druids for construction at the Chalice Well; but what the yew trees and the stories of initiation chambers reveal is the persistent association of the spring with death and rebirth.

A further suggestion made by Rahtz was that when the well shaft was first built it was a traditional medieval well house. It was, he proposed, a fairly small and square structure, which stood above ground and had a pointed stone roof. Today, the visitor looks into the building through an opening made in the roof. The evidence for the above ground well house is supported by the silting up of the valley and by the quality of the stonework. The external side of the stones in the well shaft show finishing beyond that required for something below ground. Later excavation in the area however shows that silting up around the well head is not as deep as Rahtz thought, and indeed ground nearby shows undisturbed bedrock after a foot or two. Furthermore, the stones of the well shaft that were examined might have been finished on their external faces for an original function elsewhere, i.e. the Abbey. A new reading of the evidence suggests the heading for the well built around 1200 CE may not have been a well house standing above ground, nor a shaft set deeply into the ground, but something between the two.

VESICA PISCIS

The geometrical symbol known as the *vesica piscis* was brought into Chalice Well Gardens in the early 20th century. The name originates in

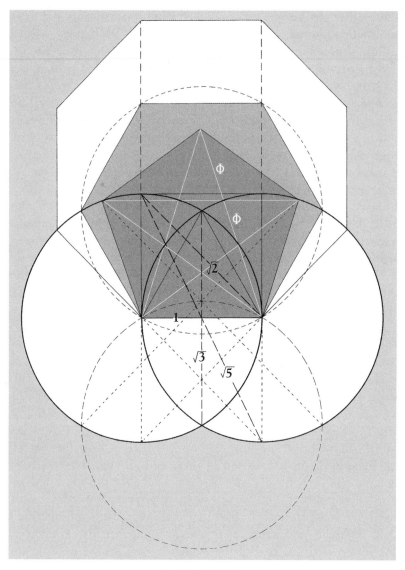

▲ Vesica Piscis

the Christian symbol of the fish (*piscis*) shaped vesica that appears when two equal overlapping circles are drawn; but this could be a way of disguising the more obvious yoni or vulva, which is how the symbol is usually described in other traditions. The vesica in Western iconography, however, is often used as a frame for sculptures of St. Mary holding her son and this does suggest recognition of the female, sexual and creative connotations of the vesica piscis in the Christian tradition.

The Vesica Piscis and the Golden Section

From the vesica piscis it is possible to generate a succession of polygons: the triangle, the square, pentagon, hexagon, octagon, decagon, dodecagon and so on. The vesica piscis provides a simple method for 'squaring the circle' and generating the square roots of 2, 3 and 5. If 1 represents the original unity as described by the line between the centres of the two circles, then $\sqrt{2}$ governs the expansion (or division) of unity in two dimensions, while $\sqrt{3}$ governs the expansion of unity in three dimensions.

The five-sided pentagon or pentacle leads directly to the ratio known as the Golden Section or *phi* (Φ). The divisions of all the lines of the pentacle are such that one section is to the other as the other is to the whole. The Golden Section describes an analogous progression of forms, numbers and volumes where the original expands (or contracts) so that the new is to the original as the original is to the whole, i.e. B is to A as A is to A plus B. This proportion or ratio is common in the natural world, where not only trees, plants and shells progress according to the Golden Section but so do the proportions of the human body: for example the arm, hand and sections of the fingers. Although it is unsatisfactory to do this, as it is a ratio not a number, *phi* can be expressed numerically as 1 to 1.618˙ or 1 to 0.618˙.

In 1772, William Preston, distinguished as 'the foremost Masonic scholar of his generation,' published *Illustrations of Masonry*. Of the Golden Section, Preston said:

> It is not only the heavens which declare the glory of God and the firmament which showeth his handiwork, but the humblest flower and the least shell which, together with the mightiest objects in the heavens, are all made and act by means of a curve developed from the Golden Section.

Plato made the Golden Section the mathematical key to the physics of the cosmos. The Egyptians considered it to be the symbol of the power that gave forth the endless series of numbers, measures and proportions – the procession of creation. It is the asymmetrical division of unity that leads to the diversity of creation and back to the symmetry of unity again. One to two to three to two to one.

19

The two interlocking circles of the vesica piscis are present in the pool built in the 1980s in the lower part of the garden. The vesica piscis with the sword of St. Michael through it is wrought in iron over the entrance to King Arthur's Courtyard. The vesica piscis is in the gates of the entranceway made in the 1990s, as well as in the stonework of the path. And finally, and perhaps most importantly, it is present on the lid, which covers the well head. Frederick Bligh Bond – the first archaeologist and architect to be in charge of the restoration of the Abbey – designed this lid as a peace offering after the 1914–18 war.

Bligh Bond was part of a Glastonbury based group of people who were interested in a new spirituality that was emerging in the West in the first part of the 20th century. This was partly due to exposure to mysticism and Eastern religions, and partly to information coming from the advance of historical understanding – largely through archaeology – of their own, native past. Bligh Bond, for example, found that the proportions generated by the vesica piscis were present in the design of Glastonbury Abbey and especially in the Mary Chapel. Other 'Avalonians', such as Alice Buckton and Dion Fortune, felt the vesica piscis symbolised the merging of different traditions, the union of spirit and matter, and the re-emergence of the feminine to achieve balance with the masculine. In 1919 the new lid on the cover of the Chalice Well was inaugurated in a ceremony that combined many different spiritual paths. It is possible that the sword of St. Michael or the 'bleeding lance' drawn through the centre of the design for the well lid was an attempt to make the symbolism of male–female balance even more explicit. When the lid required restoration in 2003, the ironwork pattern on the top of the lid was replicated upon the bottom but with some changes to the 'bleeding lance'. Hamish Miller, who was commissioned to carry out the work, turned the point of the lance into a heart.

The vesica piscis provides a simple way of arriving at the basic patterns and measures of sacred geometry, especially the fundamental ratio of the Golden Section. By drawing a circle, however crudely, perhaps with string and sticks, and then another so that the centres of each circle are on the circumference of the other, anyone can establish all the crucial ratios and numbers of sacred geometry. These are the ratios, proportions and harmonies found in nature, in the forms of plants, animals, crystals and the human body. They are also present in music and mathematics, and so form the underlying structures of creation. The vesica piscis is a powerful symbol of the creation and growth of forms in the natural world; and, given the long and successive use of Avalon as a place of death and rebirth, it is not surprising that this supremely generative symbol should appear here. It is possible to imagine the progression created by the vesica piscis endlessly unfolding in the inner dimensions of the Otherworld as much as it endlessly unfolds in the external world. The symbol is the expression of the ideal proportions of the archetypal inner world passing into visible manifestation, and the tangible proportions of the outer world returning into the realm of the eternal.

WHITE SPRING

When I first visited Glastonbury in the 1970s there was little to show that a second spring rose in the valley beside the Chalice Well. A walk past the reservoir at the bottom of Well House Lane revealed a gaping hole in the stone facade from out of which emerged sounds of dripping and running water. Enquiries led to the shrugging of shoulders and general disinterest. It was only later, in 1982, that I learnt a spring rose there, and when I discovered that it flowed from out of a cave system under the Tor – the entrance to the Otherworld – it seemed extraordinary there was little public knowledge of this spring especially when its sister spring the Chalice Well had become so famous. It was as though the spring was cloaked in a veil of silence. People did not even know its name.

▲ White Spring Reservoir

It is on record that when the building of what came to be known as the Well House Lane Reservoir was proposed in 1872, local antiquarians raised an outcry about destruction of a site steeped in historical and mythological interest. It was a popular beauty spot much frequented by locals. The antiquarians said that the stone foundations on one side of the little coombe were the remnants of a monk's cell, and that the waters of the spring coated anything they touched with a white mineral deposit. 'One thing that clings to me was the beautiful Well House Lane of those days, before it had been spoilt by the erection of the reservoir', wrote George Wright in 1894. 'The lane itself was beautiful, for the whole bank was a series of fairy dropping wells – little caverns clothed with moss and verdure, and each small twig and leaf was a medium for the water to flow, drop, drop, drop, into a small basin below. This water contained lime, and pieces of wood or leaves subject to this dropping became encrusted with a covering of lime. For a long time I attended those pretty caverns with affectionate care, and Well House Lane was an object of interest to all our visitors'.[2] Mr. Wright said the place had many traditions associated with it, that it was popularly known as the White Spring and that the public strongly protested its destruction.

The spring, or rather the springs, originally emerged out of an opening – a cave – in the coombe. This was about 18 metres (60 feet) back from the present lane and 5 metres (17 feet) above it. At one time the opening was quite large, even cavernous due to the volume of water, and went back far into the side of the Tor. It was subject to alteration due to surrounding growth, collapsing rocks and soil, and because of the concerns and attitudes of the people of the time. There is the tradition that tunnels leading back into the Tor were present in Glastonbury at the time of the monks and there are several stories recounting the misfortunes of those who entered them. In one story, thirty monks engaged in chanting in or near the Abbey grounds found a tunnel opening up before them. They entered and went in the direction of the Tor. A disaster befell them and the full story could never be obtained from the three, one struck dumb and two insane, who returned. Good reason to block off the cave!

The area suffered from cholera outbreaks in 1870 and the town council deemed it necessary to secure a safe source of water; so despite the protests, construction of the reservoir went ahead. A heading was built, the area above it back-filled and the stone reservoir was placed to fill the little coombe. To maintain the flow and quality of water the builders replaced the cave at the back of the coombe with a low, brick-lined tunnel. The last part of the tunnel, about 12 metres below the present ground level, is entirely underground. At just over 15 metres (50 feet) back from the original opening the builders ended the tunnel in a natural cave. This cave in the Blue Lias of the area can accommodate up to a dozen people. Subjected to a relatively recent collapse of the roof, further access into the cave system is now impossible.

After completing the tunnel back to this cave, the builders constructed a collection chamber, finished the reservoir and built a pump-house on top of it to create the pressure necessary to supply water to the town. Examination of the collection chamber revealed that the builders also tapped other springs apart from the White Spring. The flow of the other springs varies, and one of them deposits a very high concentration of iron. It therefore appears that an offshoot from the Chalice Well emerges beside the White Spring. This spring is particularly intermittent and sometimes stops altogether. Two other springs are also intermittent. Several springs rise on this elevation behind the houses to the south of the Tor, and further round the Tor to the east there is a substantial spring at Ashwell. Observation of these springs however shows they are entirely subject to rainfall and not of the same quality of water as the White Spring.[3]

The White Spring has a high calcium content owing to the limestone that underlies the area. On contact with matter such as leaves and twigs the water coats them with the mineral to form 'tufa'. This is a soft white stone that weighs very little due to the many holes within it caused by the eventual decay of the organic matter. There are examples of tufa in Chalice Well Gardens. They are either still in situ (in Arthur's Court) or placed where they can be seen. These might be the remnants of the formations of the White Spring. In the right conditions calcium will also create flowstone formations and even crystallise into a wide variety of forms. Examples of calcite crystals can be seen at the quarry in nearby Dulcote Hill and flowstone formations are abundant in the caves at Wookey Hole. Calcium is soluble but will precipitate rapidly to coat any surface it comes into contact with. This fact was discovered very quickly after the water came on line in 1872 and clogged the pipes of the town. Another water supply had to be found, and by the end of the 19th century up to this day all of Glastonbury's water needs are met from sources several miles to the east.

Incidentally, the water from the east – e.g. from boreholes at West Compton – is pumped up to an underground reservoir on the side of the Tor. Do not be confused, as many are, by the sound of running water under the hatch on the northeast ascent path of the Tor! Built at this elevation in 1949 to create sufficient pressure to supply Windmill Hill, the water in this 40,000 gallon two chambered reservoir is pumped here and does not have its origin on the Tor. The water in the open reservoir visible to the east of the Tor comes from the Ashwell Spring.[4]

Back then, in the early 1980s, I was certain that water-worn caves did exist in the limestone under the Tor. The legends of the tunnels and the underworld entrance implied that they were there. But it took many years of study to finally arrive at a theory that explained all the hydrological and geological phenomena of Glastonbury.

ORIGIN OF THE WATERS: THE AQUIFER

It is evident that White Spring water contains calcium, while Red Spring water is rich in iron. White Spring water emerges from the ground with little pressure, while Red Spring water makes its way upward with such force that its head is elevated three metres to make it available for drinking in the Chalice Well gardens. Measurements taken of the flow of White Spring water show that it responds rapidly to fluctuations in rainfall, while the guidebooks to the Chalice Well say the Red Spring water is constant. Although rising close together high above the water table of the surrounding land, the two springs appear to possess an entirely different nature and this makes accounting for their origin a challenge.

If the Isle of Avalon lies at the centre of a geological system capable of transporting and elevating water from far away, then the springs are examples of artesian wells originating from a distant source. This theory can account for the different qualities of the springs and for their high position below a small rainfall catchment area. An artesian well occurs when underground strata allow water to rise in one location due to the pressure created by a higher water table in another location. It is suggested for example that the waters of the Red Spring come from an iron rich area of the Mendip Hills to the north, such as Mells or Cheddar, and are carried to the Chalice Well by an artesian system. This theory accounts for the high iron content of the spring as the geology around Glastonbury contains very little iron. This origin for either spring, however, is highly unlikely, as the underlying strata do not support it. The underground strata between the Tor and the Mendips do not have the necessary structure for carrying water from one place to the other under artesian pressure. The area is underlain by heavy clay – known as Keuper Marl – which is a very poor carrier of water, and effectively seals off water rising from below. The presence of this thick layer of clay effectively rules out the distant artesian and the juvenile theories for the origin of the waters. Furthermore, geologists know that rain falling on the Mendip Hills rises at the foot of the hills and does not come to Glastonbury.[5]

If the geological evidence points to the water from the extraordinary springs being of a local and not a deep, distant origin, then this requires an extraordinary explanation. My challenge was to explain why the Red Spring rises under pressure, why it is so constant and how its mineral content differs from the White Spring when the rainfall catchment area for both springs – Glastonbury Tor – is so small and there is no iron in the area. What is the origin of two such unusual springs, when the small area of surrounding geology appears to support a local origin no more than it does a distant artesian one?

Over the years I have put the question of the origin of the springs to geologists and hydrologists. In 1992 I asked a group of them engaged in a university field project who had time on their hands due to cold and stormy weather. They spent a day considering the springs of the Isle of Avalon while I plied them with information, cake and coffee. The best, that is the most likely, theory they could come up with for the origin of the water is as follows. (If the reader does not wish to work their way through the evidence now, please go directly to the following section 'Under the Tor' where the material is summarised.)

A very long time ago, what was to become this part of the world was an ocean floor receiving vast amounts of sediment. Over millions of years, thick and contrasting layers of sediment accumulated. On the bottom – or the bottom of the relevant geology – were the Lias beds laid down in the Jurassic age (208–146 million years ago). These beds included clays, marlstone (the Keuper Marl), and the limestone known as Blue Lias used to build the houses in this part of Somerset to this day. Above these beds was deposited a layer of soft yellow stone, known as Midford Sandstone. It is this sandstone that forms the Tor and the other hills in the area, such as Pennard Hill to the east, today. This sandstone layer is spread throughout the region and in places reaches a depth of 80 metres (250 ft). Above that were yet more layers of a varied nature and, this is the significant part, at least one of them contained huge quantities of iron. This iron-rich layer was likely to have appeared very red. I use past tense here, as these layers, laid down after about 160 million years ago, are no longer in existence. Even though geologists know they were here – and one of these layers, known as Oxford Clay, was likely to have been over 150 metres thick – all of them have eroded away from this part of the world.

▲ **Torr Burr.** A Tor Burr lies exposed in the Midford Sandstone on the southern flank of the Tor. The Ordnance Survey Map of 1902 locates another, now missing, stone nearby. It is likely to have rolled down the Tor. This remaining stone was shored up in 2003 to avoid the same fate. The stones are said to be the eggs of dragons. They were once so numerous in the fields of the area they were used for the foundations of buildings including the Abbey. They are formed by the action of iron-rich water leaching into sandstone. The location of this example marks the spot where the labyrinth is said to make its final turn 'into' the Tor.

As conditions changed and as land masses shifted over the next hundred million years, these layers lifted upwards to form a plateau. Rain falling on this plateau drained easily into the soft underlying stone and in places erosion formed gorges and long valleys. In some places water flowing downwards from the surface of the plateau carried the minerals from the upper layers into the lower. Fissures formed, and caves and tunnels were created in the lower limestone layers. Over many millions of years the iron present in the upper layers leached into the water and was deposited in the lower layers of sand and shale. As the iron rich water passed into the Midford layers it hardened the sandstone and in places caused even harder nodules to form. These nodules, or Tor Burrs as they are called, range in size from less than a centimetre to the metre long 'eggstone' behind the Abbot's kitchen in the Abbey grounds.

Over time the top layers of red, iron-bearing stone were entirely eroded away and erosion began on the layer of Midford Sandstone. The ice ages eroded and smoothed the land still further, but where the iron rich water from the earlier epochs had infiltrated and hardened the sandstone it resisted erosion, and so began to appear the familiar landscape of the present day. Glastonbury Tor emerged as the hardened sandstone that forms its core resisted erosion while the softer stone around it wore away. Tor Burrs littered the land as a result of this process, and were used as foundations in the building of the Abbey. Within and forming the Tor, however, remains an aquifer, a water bearing system created in earlier times when large amounts of water filtered through from above. The bottom part of this aquifer, in the heavier and impervious shales and limestones, is heavily saturated with iron.

Professor O. T. Jones describes how this type of process takes place. The erosion of 'iron-bearing shales, which stood at that time at a higher elevation than the surrounding limestone', he said in an address to the British Association, 'led to the release of the pyrites, which on oxidation gave rise to acidic iron-bearing waters. It was probably due to the activity of such waters passing over the limestone . . . that the ore in the limestone was formed. Similar waters . . . would furnish the necessary iron content to those sediments'.[6]

This theory about the origin of the Tor seemed coherent to me. It fitted the known information, even though it differs from the opinion of the Tor archaeologist Philip Rahtz. He suggested an iron-hardening action, but from water coming from an artesian spring (i.e. the Red Spring) below the Tor not from above it.[7] But even if I had the true picture of how the Tor was formed, it was the aquifer – the water bearing system – that I really needed to get to grips with in order to understand the behaviour of the Red and White Springs issuing from the Tor.

The aquifer within the Tor, the university geologists explained, has larger features than merited by the amount of rainfall the area now

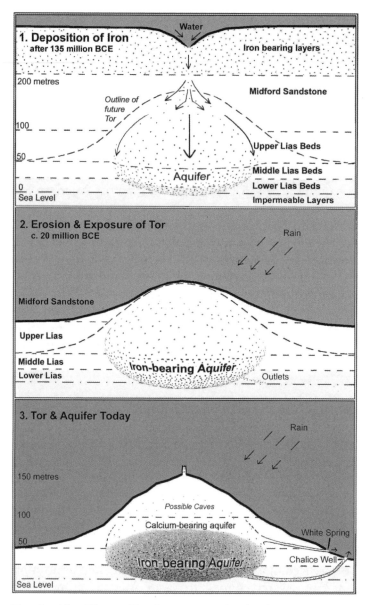

1. Deposition of Iron
after 135 million BCE

Water

Iron bearing layers

200 metres

Outline of future Tor

Midford Sandstone

100

50

Upper Lias Beds

Middle Lias Beds

Aquifer

Lower Lias Beds

0
Sea Level

Impermeable Layers

2. Erosion & Exposure of Tor
c. 20 million BCE

Rain

Midford Sandstone

Upper Lias

Middle Lias
Lower Lias

Iron-bearing Aquifer

Outlets

3. Tor & Aquifer Today

Rain

150 metres

Possible Caves

100

Calcium-bearing aquifer

White Spring

50

Iron-bearing Aquifer

Chalice Well

Sea Level

▲ **The Tor Aquifer.** The aquifer that accounts for the shape of the Tor can be envisaged as a huge underground chamber full of sediment and saturated with water. This chamber was created long ago when the volume of water in the system was much greater and minerals from the now vanished layers above – especially iron – were deposited into it. The aquifer has calcium rich layers at the top and much denser iron saturated layers at the base. An impermeable layer of heavy clay seals the chamber from below. The water level in the aquifer is maintained by rain falling upon the Tor and it is regulated by water flowing from the springs. The water of the White Spring flows from off the top of the aquifer: it responds rapidly in the manner of an overflow to the rainwater coming in and it is rich in calcium.

The water of the Red Spring comes from the base of the aquifer or chamber in quite a different manner. The water remains in the airless veins of the aquifer for a considerable length of time and gathers up the iron and other minerals there. The water of the spring flows out evenly and under artesian pressure because of the amount of water in the Tor aquifer above it and because its outlet is restricted. The water flows out through a fissure in the otherwise impervious underlying strata that has the effect of a narrow pipe. It is conceivable that if this 'pipe' was widened or lowered all the water would drain out of the aquifer, or if the pipe was raised high enough no water would flow out of it at all. The water would flow out of the other outlet – the overflow at the White Spring. This is what happens at times of maximum pressure in the system when the collection chamber by the White Spring sees an increase in the flow of an iron-rich spring located there.

receives. This is because it was made when the location was a catchment for a greater supply of water from above, that is, from strata now eroded away. It is likely, they thought, that the climate at the time was far wetter, even tropical, and this would account for the volume of water. Subsequent research bore this out when plate tectonics revealed this part of the world was moving north over the tropics during this period – indeed Britain is still moving north, toward the Arctic, today. The upper parts of the aquifer lie in the Midford Sandstone and the upper layers of Lias, and these are likely to include a subterranean network of caves created by the once greater volume of acidic iron-bearing water pouring downwards into them. The top of the aquifer lies in the Tor high above the present exit point of the White Spring, which is about 15 metres above that of the Red Spring. The lower part of the aquifer lies in the lower layers of Lias into which have leached tremendous quantities of iron. This layer lies deep in the Tor from above the exit point of the Red Spring and descends into the iron rich layers that lie lower than the spring. Rain falling on the Tor is sufficient to keep the aquifer saturated and, because of its size and the impervious clay layers below, the aquifer does not dry up.

When it rains heavily on the Tor some water is discharged by surface springs, but other water finds its way into the aquifer. The caves in the top layers of the aquifer fill up and quickly discharge their water – within a week or so – into the White Spring. During dryer times the water on the top of the aquifer is discharged at a much slower rate of flow. I discuss the important matter of rate of flow in a moment. The water picks up the calcium present in the limestone layers easily and deposits these at the White Spring. Examples of springs like the White Spring can be seen on nearby hills with similar geology. On Pennard Hill, the springs that carry calcium deposit it in places as huge tufa formations.

The water that lies in the lower layers of the aquifer, however, has a quite different character. It is filtered by the much denser nature of the sediment in the lower layers, and it carries little calcium; indeed, any calcium is filtered out. Instead, it picks up the iron that leached into the lower layers over an immense period of geological time, and the mineral rich water is released under pressure from the bottom of the constantly full aquifer. Below it is the thick impervious clay of the Lower Lias Beds and this does not allow the water to pass through to the surrounding water table of the Levels. It is possible that once upon a time when the volume of water was much greater these layers did allow the water to pass through, and this accounts for the presence of tunnels below Chalice Hill toward the Abbey. But as the volume of water flowing through the system diminished, these tunnels were not kept clear, they collapsed, and the head of the spring gravitated higher up. The conclusion is that, due to the weight of water in the aquifer above, and because the water cannot pass out through the clay below, the water rises upward to emerge under the fairly constant artesian pressure, temperature and volume characteristic of the Red Spring at the Chalice Well.[8]

The Red Spring although fed by the same aquifer, does not fluctuate like the White Spring as its rate of flow is determined by the relatively stable volume of water in the aquifer as a whole and by the dense nature of the minerals through which it flows. As the aquifer reaches maximum saturation in winter months the volume of water at the Chalice Well does increase slightly, however, and in the summer months it decreases. The maximum flow of the Chalice Well in winter is around 25,000 gallons per day (gpd), while in summer it drops to around 19,000 gpd.[9] This is consistent with local rainfall patterns and so supports the case for a local rather than a distant artesian or juvenile origin for the water. The temperature of the water is also consistent with the springs of the area. This makes a juvenile origin unlikely as the deeper source of this water tends to give it a higher temperature.

According to the Water Board, the White Spring 'rises in the Midford Sands overlying the upper Lias beds' on the Tor and 'flows from the heading in Tor Hill', which they call Tor Springs or Well

House Spring. Measurements made as long ago as the 19th century say the rate of flow of the spring fluctuates from a minimum of 4,500 gpd to a maximum of over 70,000 gpd. Measurements made more recently show it has an average flow of about 10,000 gpd, and in the seven years from the late 1980s into the mid 1990s it never reached the maximum figure. In the spring of 1994 for example, after a very wet winter, the peak flow of the White Spring was 22,000 gpd. The maximum flow

---

The Volume of Water Supplying the Aquifer

In wet months the Tor acts as giant sponge soaking up rainfall. The cool climate and the grass on the Tor mean there is little erosion and little water loss through evaporation and run off. Although approximately one half of the rain that falls on the Tor is lost through evaporation, the remainder percolates into its depths. The area of ground specifically covered by the Tor is about 360,000 square yards, but the surrounding land increases the effective surface area to over 500,000 square yards (418,000 square metres), or one sixth of a square mile. Given average rainfall in the region to be 26 inches (66 cm) per year, then after allowing one half for loss, 100,000–150,000 gallons (450–680 thousand litres) of water per day can be expected to flow from the aquifer within the Tor, depending on the season.

The top of the aquifer is likely to lie about 100 ft (30 m) below the summit of the Tor (518 ft or 160 m above sea level). The springs emerge 250 ft below this at about 160 ft (50 m) above sea level. The bottom of the aquifer, from where the waters of the Red Spring derive, permeates deeper than this however to the Lower Lias clay at about 100 ft (30 m) above sea level. The total depth of the aquifer is therefore about 320 ft (100 m). Given an area of 500,000 square yards, a depth of 106 yards, and allowing for a conical shape, I estimate the volume of the aquifer to be over 25 million cubic yards (19 million cubic metres). The volume of water coming from the springs represents about 100th of 1 percent of the aquifer's total capacity, or about a cup of water to every square yard of rock and soil. With iron-bearing water accounting for about half of this amount there is plenty of time for it to sit in the system, absorb the iron, stabilise its temperature and emerge in a slightly varying seasonal flow at the Chalice Well.

from all the springs that meet in the collection chamber beside the White Spring, plus the Chalice Well, plus other springs immediately around the Tor including the spring at Ashwell, was estimated at 100,000 gpd during the spring of that year. As the Water Board tapped a number of these springs to fill the Well House Lane Reservoir, this could account for their original high estimate.

Taking the average rainfall for Glastonbury to be twenty-six inches per year and assuming the catchment area of the White Spring to be the Tor, or about one sixth of a square mile, then following the standard equation employed by the Water Board that allows for one half loss by evaporation and run off, the maximum volume of water to be expected emerging from the area covered by the Tor is in the region of 125,000 gpd. This amount agrees with the average annual volume of the Chalice Well, 18,000 gpd, plus the average annual volume of the White Spring, 10,000 gpd, plus the potential maximum of all other springs in the area, 90,000–100,000 gpd.[10] These figures confirm that the catchment area formed by the Tor above the Red and White Springs is sufficient to supply their waters. Indeed, a spring averaging 20,000 gpd needs an area of less then 250 square yards to supply it in typical British conditions!

The theory of the geology and the aquifer of the Tor that I have developed here is supported by this evidence. It provides an explanation that accounts for the origin, the mineral nature and the mineral difference between the two springs. The waters of the springs are, in effect, 'home brewed'. They do not originate from far away. The waters originate from an aquifer created in highly unusual circumstances below the Tor and, in fact, they created the Tor and give it the shape it has today.

UNDER THE TOR

As this research developed, I began to realise that the geological theory describing the origin of the springs beneath the Tor might provide me with a geophysical reason for the long held power of Avalon. The theories of the geologists put me in a position to accurately see within the Tor for the first time.

In summary, the Tor is an iron impregnated sandstone and limestone hill underlain by impervious beds of marlstone and clay. The whole contains an aquifer. The upper part of this aquifer includes fissures and tunnels, while the lower part consists of a much deeper and denser bed into which has leached tremendous amounts of iron. This aquifer was formed many millions of years ago when the land mass overhead and the volume of water and minerals contained in the system were much greater. The mineral-bearing water in the layers above percolated downwards to harden the lower layers into an unusual three-dimensional subterranean formation. With the erosion of the overlying landmass, the hardened layers formed the conical hill that now dramatically towers above a surrounding level plain. The aquifer that made the Tor is still within it, but on a reduced scale. The hill, the aquifer and its mineral content, form a core with unusual energetic properties. Scientific models show that when water flows under pressure through the dense veins of a subterranean aquifer, its atoms generate a positive charge in relation to the negative charge of water not under pressure nearer the surface.

So far so good, but there are other ways than conventional science to see within things. Traditional systems of geomancy for example describe the Tor as an elevation containing a core saturated with water around which vortex energies resembling a sevenfold dragon coil. These energies possess an outward-turning, centrifugal or negative polarity and an inward-turning, centripetal or positive polarity. The waters of the Red Spring come from the bottom of the system where the densest quantity of iron is stored. These waters flow at a fairly constant pressure and provide the connection with the positive polarity of the coil. The waters of the White Spring come from the top of the system. They fluctuate widely according to the amount of water in the system, and provide the connection to the negative polarity of the coil. The waters are like the two different solutions of an electric battery, while the iron impregnated mineral layers of the hill form the plates.

Traditional geomancy develops this case still further by pointing out that the core is also magnetic as it contains iron. There is an electrical circuit and a magnetic circuit. These currents form sheaves around the Tor of polarised, opposing and attracting energy. The energies vary according to the state of the aquifer; becoming more magnetic in dry conditions when the top of the aquifer is relatively low, and more electric when the aquifer is full and the White Spring is flowing fully. The terraces act to synchronise with and enhance the currents of subtle electromagnetic energy created by the iron and water-filled core. I explore these properties fully in the final section of this book.

The aquifer below the Tor is a huge one made in an earlier age, and merely needs topping up to maintain its level. Several dowsers informed me that the top of an aquifer of this nature possesses a 'dome' that is held in place by pressure. If the pressure is lost then the dome can fall; an experience often met by those drilling for water. Fortunately the

The Crystal Resonance Chamber in the Tor

In 1995 I accompanied a Somerset water dowser to the Tor and recorded her impressions. The Water Board unofficially recommended her to me. Her particular interest lay in the interaction between minerals and underground water. She had successfully 'trapped', directed and purified springs through the placement of stones and crystals, and found the configuration of dowsable energy patterns upon the Tor similar to those she had achieved artificially. She attributed this to the subterranean arrangement of stones and minerals.

She said a 'crystal resonance chamber' lay directly below the summit of the Tor that has the effect of amplifying the energy field of the aquifer. 'The aquifer', she said, 'creates an energy field aligned vertically and horizontally in every direction. Two main currents, rather like spirals, wind their way through this field, upwards and downwards, inwards and outwards'. One of the currents had a 'yin' charge, the other a 'yang' charge. When asked to explain her terms, she said those were the names she gave to earth energies according to their feminine and masculine attributes. She felt the two currents – which are common over water domes or 'blind springs' – achieved 'an exceptional fusion because the spatial arrangement of the aquifer capped by the crystalline chamber allowed them to align and dance in greater resonance'.

She thought the chamber and passages below the summit of the Tor must contain crystallised minerals other than calcite for them to have this effect on the energy. The calcite may be impregnated with iron crystals, perhaps pyrites, if not quartz. She divined the presence of a layer of 'nodules' corresponding to the iron rich Tor Burrs or eggstones that fill the Tor. 'It must be a fairyland', she said, 'of stalagmites, stalactites, dendrites, flowstones, crystals, geodes and nodules within there'.

'What is extraordinary is that the energy structure created by the invisible water should be so perfectly apparent in the visible. What you see on the outside is what you get on the inside. Even the terraces reveal the internal structure of the aquifer. I have never seen anything like it. . . . It is as though a natural energy dynamic has created the aquifer, mineral formations and the external profile of the Tor, which in turn create it'.

aquifer below the Tor is held in place by the nature of the stone and soil. There is plenty of sticky clay in the marlstone below the Midford Sandstone that tends to allow only small cavities to form before resealing itself. The opening to the White Spring for example bears witness to this. It is unstable, and cavities formed by the flow of water need shoring up as they soon collapse.

The layers of sandstone and limestone near the top of the aquifer have hollow cavities and tunnels that feature crystalline and flowstone formations. Calcite crystallises easily and there are many remarkable examples of calcite crystals found in the surrounding area. Dendrites and flowstone curtains have formed in the passage and reservoir of the White Spring built in the 1870s. Legend says there was access from here under the Tor itself, but this way is now closed. As described above, any tunnels and chambers that do exist under the Tor are most likely to lie on the top of the aquifer directly beneath the summit. Dowsers claim that crystalline formations interact with and affect the energy patterns formed by flowing underground water.

THE NATURAL VALLEY

The small valley between Chalice Hill and the Tor became increasingly important for my understanding of the energies of the Tor because of the springs that rise there. Armed with a theory that accounted for the origin and nature of the springs, my investigations began at the Red Spring or Chalice Well on the assumption that the waters of the spring originally issued out of the ground from a fissure in the bedrock. This assumption proved correct, and it was intriguing to learn that the engineer who capped the well in 1958 described not just one but two springs emerging from the bedrock. One spring had less volume than the other, but the engineer thought it likely they shared the same source.[11]

The spring rises on a level dominated by the Middle Lias beds of the area. Above these are the Upper Lias beds, and above them is the Midford Sandstone of the Tor. These beds were laid down between 360 and 65 million years ago as sediment on the floor of a mostly tropical sea.[12] The small valley in which the springs lie was created by the erosive effect of water on such soft stone, while harder stones such as Tor Burrs and Blue Lias have washed into it. The gardeners at the Chalice Well find many stones embedded with ammonites, demonstrating the origin of the stone from seas long ago.

The original profile of the valley was deeper than it is now and V-shaped in its upper and middle part. Where the valley opens up, detritus from above was deposited and the ground levels off. The water in the valley came from four sources: surface run-off, a spring higher up the valley, the White Spring and the Chalice Well. The higher spring now only flows in winter during wet periods so it is linked to surface run-off, but not so long ago it must have flowed continuously to maintain the watercress that was cultivated in beds that can be seen there.

Around 2,000 years ago, the small valley with its busy stream flowing in a narrow, deeply cut and stony cleft was filled with plants and overhung by trees. The bottom of the cleft was kept clear by the action of the water, while the Chalice Well deposited an iron rich sediment on any stones and vegetation it touched from that point downward. Shortly below this, where the valley begins to broaden and deposition occurred, the water of the White Spring made its entry. This water left a thick deposit of 'tufa' on the eastern slope up to the Tor. Tufa is a light, white rock full of holes where organic matter caught in the sediment has decayed. Whereas the waters of the upper valley combined with the Chalice Well tended towards a flushing action, at this point the waters of the White Spring added to the deposit fanning outward at the base of the valley.

Even though the view from below was obscured by vegetation, it is possible to imagine the original scene. A narrow but brilliant flash of the red streambed comes directly down the valley overhung by the dark green of yew trees. Mosses and ferns are thick on the ground. Coming in from the upper right hand side is a streambed of white that tends to form pools in bulbous formations of greyish white soft stone. The water falls over these formations, around horsetails, Hart's Tongue ferns and other plants, before joining with the waters of the Red Spring.

Where the two springs join, the ground is fairly level and accessible for the first time. Over the years animals and humans have made their way to drink here. They have made pools to ease convenience of drinking before the stream falls away down the increased slope below and into the surrounding marshland. A path comes in from both sides to reach the water, and it is likely this path is preserved both in fact and in name by Chilkwell Street: the 'chalk well street'. Unless this a corruption of the Latin *chalybeis* meaning iron, or, less likely, the Greek *chalkos* for copper, the name derives from the White Spring, as a dominant feature at the time was the chalky tufa formation created by the White Spring.

The tufa formations lie on the right hand side of the valley. They reach overhead in a myriad collection of little pools, smooth and

▲ White Spring restored

rounded slopes, vegetation covered inclines and dripping falls. At the top, the source of the bulbous formations becomes clear: although water emerges from several places, there is a single main source that is responsible for them. This water issues from a cave that runs back under the Tor and is aligned with its NE–SW axis. The water flows along the floor of the fairly level cave and it can be followed back until the lowness of the roof makes it no longer possible. The air is a little stale and noxious, but the taste of the water is pleasant. It is of the temperature and quality found in the springs of the limestone hills in the area.

The thick vegetation in the base of the coombe hampers the way to the source of the Red Spring. Even though the overhanging yew trees make it quite dark, vegetation still thrives in the moist conditions, and in summer there are stinging nettles. Early in the year, however, ferns and mosses dominate the way. It is dark in here and very green, and the vivid red streambed, smooth in places from centuries of deposition of iron, is choked in other places by fallen stones and by rapidly dis-colouring branches, twigs and decaying leaves. Where scouring action does not erode them away – behind rocks, attached to branches and to the leaves of dipping plants – long fingers of red algae grow. These clumps, like those clotting blood, should be avoided, for they are very slippery.

Through a last dark thicket of yew lies a small, steeply sided hollow. Water gushes upward from the bottom of a small bank of rocks and stones. The water bubbles out from either side of a large stone, making it seem there are two sources. The pool in the centre of the hollow is a solid mass of red algae, gently swaying in the flow. The bank itself is about four or five feet high, and a small amount of water flows over it from the valley above. It is evident that if the ground water coming from the valley above could be kept apart, the spring would be an excel-lent supply of drinking water. It is also a true spring, not just a seepage spring, as it is cool and emerges under steady artesian pressure from a source, a mineral full aquifer, deep below the surface of the earth.

It is clear that this is an iron spring, chalybeate, full of dissolved iron salts, haematite. The name 'blood spring' comes easily to mind, especially where the algae forms stringy nodes resembling clotting blood. It is as though an artery of the living body of the earth comes to the surface here. With the two dramatic hills on both sides, and the sister spring, the white down below, the place is certainly unusual. It is set apart in such a way that it is probably dedicated to the sacred by the peoples of this era, if not to the deities of life and death themselves.

BRONZE AND IRON AGES

If it were possible to view the valley in the Celtic Iron Age, what would have accompanied the natural scene? The Celtic tribes of the area venerated the island, and as they worshipped in groves and beside springs in general, and saw this valley in particular as the entrance to the Otherworld, how would they have embellished it?

There is a track advancing along what is now Chilkwell Street from the direction of the town, and beside it is a watering system for the animals kept upon the island. To prevent these animals from entering the valley itself there is a hedge, and just before this are the water tanks. The grazing animals of the island drink here, as well as the animals of any visitors, and the visitors themselves. This situation persisted for a millennium. Provision was always made at the foot of the valley for the animals of those coming to the island on business, for the annual fairs, for pleasure, or for pilgrimage. Having made the long haul from the springs on Pennard Hill, over the causeway across the Levels and up the long eastern flank of the island, it was a relief to arrive at the cool and copious supply of water provided by the little valley below the Tor. In later years, the Abbey sought to control this supply, or at least make sure everyone received what they were entitled to; and at busy times like fairs, drinking troughs on hard standing were provided.

Back in prehistory, the track turns into the valley and runs before some circular buildings that face south on ground made level at the base of Chalice Hill. Evidence for the buildings comes from the discovery of a posthole in the ground approximately where the main buildings of Chalice Well Trust stand today. This is a prime habitation site, and radiocarbon analysis from the remains of the post indicated that some kind of structure was there since at least the Bronze Age.[13] No more is known about the structure than this, and given the tiny amount of other Bronze Age finds on the site, or indeed upon the island as a whole, it is absolutely impossible to argue from the evidence exactly what it was. It is however possible to argue precisely from the lack of evidence that given the density of Neolithic, Mesolithic, Bronze and Iron Age sites and populations in the surrounding area, the people of those eras did not come to live here. When they did come here it was because they held the island in especial reverence. They came because of some sacred and ritual purpose.

It is well known that by the Iron Age, the Somerset Levels lay on the borders of three main tribal groupings. The Romans called these tribes

The King of the Summerland

In the Arthurian romances, the King of the Summerland is called Melwas. He abducts Guinevere and holds her in his Tor-top stronghold until Arthur rescues her through the intervention of the Abbey. The importance of this account by Caradoc of Llancarfan is that it firmly places Arthur in Avalon from the 12th century and not much more was ever derived from the story than this until it is viewed in the light of the Otherworld traditions of the soul portal. Melwas is a Cornish variant on Gwynn ap Nudd, Guinevere is a solar goddess and the Summerland is a Celtic name for the Otherworld. The story preserves a memory of the pre-Christian traditions of the Otherworld.

A fundamental aspect of pre-Christian (read pre-Columbian etc.) traditions is that the figures later described in a Classical or Christian context as male 'Gods' are often guides to death and the underworld. Melwas/Gwynn is a doorkeeper, a Guardian of the Threshold, a ferryman or psychopomp, the 'conductor of souls' to the realms of the dead. Such figures appear in ancient tradition as the guardian and protector concerned for the well being of the soul undertaking the journey of birth, life and death. As Leader of the Wild Hunt, as King of the Fairies, as son and lover of Arianrhod, as son of Nudd (Nodens) King of the Underworld, and 'in whom', says the *Mabinogion*, 'is set the energy of the demons of Annwn', Gwynn fights with his perpetual rival, Gwythyr ap Greidyawl. They compete for the hand of the Solar 'Goddess' Creiddylad. As a chthonian King of the Waning Year, Gwynn returns to the earth at Beltane in a boat-shaped oak coffin, allowing Gwythyr to rule over the Waxing Year. Gwynn re-emerges six months later at Samhain when he guides the riders of the Wild Hunt – and their hounds, the red and white *Cwm Annwn* – to seek out the souls of the deceased. He then escorts the dead to the Gates of the Otherworld. The origins of Gwynn probably lay in his role as a Neolithic mortuary deity – the Lord of the Necropolis – where he and his kin presided over every hollow hill and mound of the Otherworld folk, the Sidhe.

It is likely that, if a pagan temple ever adorned the summit of the Tor, this is the figure to whom it was dedicated. His partner was the sun: perhaps known as Sulis and remembered in Creiddylad, Guinevere and possibly in Brigit or Bride. (For an alternative interpretation of this legend see Appendix 2.)

the Dobunni, the Durotiges and the Dumnonii. Although the Durotiges to the southeast enjoyed considerable wealth and a greater degree of hierarchical and centralised leadership, these tribes were essentially self-governing, autonomous and decentralised sub-chiefdoms.[14] The Levels occupied a neutral area between them; and the Tor stood out at the centre of this liminal territory, visible to them all. None could claim it; so it stood apart – best accessed by boat – available as special ground to the people of southwest Britain.

A remarkable piece of evidence that reveals the people of this period used the Isle of Avalon as an isle of the dead is the discovery of a Bronze Age burial 11 miles away at a site near Cadbury Castle. There a body was placed in a tapered boat-like container over 2.5 metres long with its ends directly aligned to Glastonbury Tor. The archaeologist Robert Tabor suggested the burial showed 'that the dead may have been journeying to that island rising from the Somerset Levels at around 1700 BC, long before any Arthur!'[15]

The Bronze Age structure on the Isle of Avalon was especially built for the purpose of people coming to the springs. It may have been a dwelling for a guardian of the grove and springs, but it may be something other than this. Given the bogginess of the ground below, the steepness of the hills above and the density of the trees within the valley, the only clear and fairly level area for an assembly of people in the valley is here. So the most likely scenario is that this area on the side of Chalice Hill was developed to provide space for people to assemble, prepare themselves and briefly stay during periods of ritual activity in the grove beside the springs.

The site of the grove – the centre of ritual activity – is beside the confluence of the two springs, where the valley widens and levels off. This is the area around the two large yew trees in Chalice Well Gardens today. From here, the celebrants and initiates could visit the emergence places of the two springs and the other areas of ritual activity. Paths lead to the cave at the White Spring and to the deep secluded hollow at the Blood Spring. These places were adorned and provided with features such as fire pits, altars, waterspouts and bathing pools. It is hard to be certain exactly what features were provided as little has been found and the priests and priestesses of the Celts, the Druids, preferred natural places for worship, not artificial ones. The golden rule of the Isle of Avalon was nothing added, nothing built, only temporary structures and features that rapidly returned to the natural state.

Deep in the sacred grove, however, there are objects hanging on the trees. Like the objects at holy wells today they are supplications, votive offerings. They are gestures from the living to the ancestors – messages

Ponter's Ball

Ponter's Ball is a huge eastward facing ditch and earth bank over a kilometre in length. It cuts across the causeway that was the only dry connection between the original island and the mainland. The ditch, when full of water, cut off and controlled access to the island. The name originates from the Latin *pontis vallum*, which means the 'bridge over the ditch'; but the earthwork is earlier than the Latin speaking medieval monks or even the Romans, and is far more in keeping with the earthworks built in the Bronze and Iron Ages for defensive and boundary marking purposes. Excavators thought the few Iron Age pottery shards, 800–100 BCE, indicated the most likely time of construction; but the working of the ditch at a later date indicated the boundary to control the traffic going to and from the Isle of Avalon was maintained for many centuries through the 'Arthurian' and Anglo-Saxon periods up until and during the time of Glastonbury Abbey.

If Ponter's Ball was originally Iron Age the Celtic people were going to uncharacteristic trouble to defend an area of little strategic or economic value. Very little from the Iron Age has been found on the island, although there was plenty of activity nearby. It may be that a herd of cattle or horses was kept upon the island, and these animals were deemed special enough to merit the effort of such a monumental boundary. The native cattle of the area are either red or white. It may be that the Celts felt the island was worthy of such bold demarcation for reasons of sanctuary or sanctity. In either case Ponter's Ball was a *temenos* – a ritual boundary separating the outside world from the sanctified land within. When the ditch was first filled the island became entirely ringed by water and so fulfilled its spiritual and symbolic role.

The ditch ensured that the journey to Avalon as the Gateway between the Worlds was best made by boat. The water that now entirely surrounded the island and was the vital essence of its soul portal became its means of transport and protection. The oak boat of its ferryman, Gwynn or Melwas, guided by the fairy lights of the marshes, plied its trade in souls. The Celts, famous for their fearlessness in death and their belief in auspicious and often instantaneous rebirth, maintained the island for this purpose. The earthwork kept the mundane pastoral herds, the farmers and traders out. Perhaps only the smiths, with their otherworldly role, were allowed in (as attested by the Iron Age forges on the 'mount' to the west of the island near Beckery). Perhaps, on a more sinister note, Ponter's Ball controlled the members of the school upon the island, making certain that the work of soul transference only focused upon those the dominant powers wished to be reborn!

▲ The bridge and gateway at Ponter's Ball around the fifth century CE. It is possible that a circular temple existed on the Tor at this time. Little has been found from this period, but the high numbers of bones from choice cuts of meat found in fissures on the summit of the Tor suggest either a garrison or the practice of sacrificial offering.[31] Drawing by Alan Royce.

to the spirits of the place, and to the greater powers of life and death. However, they are quite unlike the objects thrown into many pools and rivers by the Celtic peoples: swords, shields, chariot fittings, pins, brooches and other decorative metal pieces. These are softer, perishable items of cloth, leather, sinew, wood, bone, flowers, woven grasses and straw. They are meant to dissolve into the environment; and besides, if objects of value were deposited here someone else would retrieve them as the pools have little depth. No, the place to leave those more valuable offerings was in the depths of the waters surrounding the island. They were, for example, thrown into the water near today's Pomparles Bridge, where the river runs through a narrow strait, keeping a deep channel clear. This, the 'Perilous Bridge', is of course exactly the place where tradition tells us Bedivere returned Excalibur to the waters of the lake. The 'Pontplerus' of Arthurian legend – described by Leland in 1542 – may retain ancient memories of the practice of offering large valuable objects like swords to the waters beside the sacred island of Avalon.[16]

Although the waters surrounding this Isle of the Dead may also have received the bones, if not the bodies of the deceased, the offerings left beside the springs at the heart of the island are appropriate for ritual practices of transition. Here, the objects left on the trees and beside the spring are impermanent and suggest transformation: a lock of hair, an entire head of hair, bloody rags, bones, ashes – items the gardeners of Chalice Well still find deposited by the springs today.

A yew tree that grew in the valley was cut down and chopped up with metal axes in the Roman era. What was unusual was that instead of being used – for yew has high utility value – the two foot high stump remained in the ground until covered in silt, as though no one dared come to collect it. Could this be evidence of the Romans destroying a sacred grove? The yew was found in a trench cut just above the gate behind the well, at a depth of about 12 feet. This gives a good idea of the ground level at the base of the coombe about 2000 years ago.[17]

CELTIC AVALON

The name 'Avalon' is given to many locations. Investigation reveals that these locations all have certain qualities in common. Each is, in some way, an island, surrounded by water. They possess a high feature, such as a hill. They usually have a remarkable tree, from which come special fruits, and emblematic creatures. They all have an entranceway: a cave, a doorway, a bridge, or a pass into the high place. They often lie to the west of the cultural area of which they are a part and the traditions of that culture reveal they function in a similar way. They are the entranceway to and the exit from the Otherworld. The Otherworld is the dwelling place of the soul before birth and after death.

The idea of 'Avalon' as the entrance to the Otherworld is not unique to Britain. There are 'Avalons' all over the world. An Avalon for example is found in the Chinese Taoist traditions surrounding Ming Hill. Located beside the city of Fengdu on the Yangtze River, the 288 metre terraced hill is known as the 'City of Ghosts'. It is the place souls go to after death. They meet an impartial judge, a 'King of Hell', who reveals the different realms they may enter. The origins of such Avalons lie in the past. The Taoist tradition around Ming Hill is first recorded almost 2000 years ago. The Buddhist teaching on the Western 'Pure Land' is thought to be even older. In Britain it is hard to know when the tradition was first established, but the Celtic culture in Britain seems entirely familiar with the Avalonian soul portal.

For the Celtic peoples, Avalon was an island in the west that provided access between the worlds. Many places served in this way. The large body of surviving early Irish literature says that Avalon is an island in the western sea, and it had many names such as *Tír na n'Óg,* the Land of Youth and *Tír na mBeo,* the Land of the Living. It was reached by crossing a plain – the Plain of Honey, or *Magh Mhór,* the Great Plain. In the Celtic worldview, there is no creator outside of and before creation, so there is no Celtic creation mythology and no dualism of earth and spirit. The immortal soul dwells forever in a universe that has neither a beginning nor an end. Although the true home of the soul is in the realm of the immortals, the soul incarnates again and again. The soul dwells in a *tuirgin,* a circuit of births or existences: '...a birth that passes from every nature into another ... a transitory birth which has traversed all nature...'[18]

This continuous process of rebirth, or metempsychosis, means the soul is present in animate and inanimate forms. Celtic bards such as Amergin and Taliesin describe the presence of their souls in every form of existence:

> *I am the wind upon the sea*
> *I am the wave upon the ocean*
> *I am the murmur of the strand*
> *I am a stag of seven points...*[19]

There is little suggestion of a progression or a hierarchy of incarnation in the Celtic worldview. It is not better to be human. The point is to experience every form of incarnation. There is evidence to suggest that the incarnation of the soul is aspectual. That is, only an aspect of the soul incarnates in form while the true nature of the eternal soul is only in full evidence in the Otherworld. It is here, where there is 'no sickness, no suffering and no death' that the soul exists with full awareness and presence.[20]

Due to the constant cycle of soul incarnation in the Celtic worldview everything is alive with presence. The soul of life is the life of the soul, and vice versa. Not only are humans, animals and plants full of soul or spirit, but so are inanimate and intangible things like a breeze, a ray of light or a word. Aspects of the soul may also incarnate in other worlds, such as the fairy realm, the Land of the Sidhe, but this is not considered desirable as the fairy world is full of illusion. Finally, the presences of soul can group together. That is, they share a common energy or character, which in the Celtic world belonged to the realm of the ancestors. A particular ancestral presence dwelt within certain forms, which then expressed this quality in their lives. An individual could embody this quality, and it was closely related to the idea of the 'sovereignty' of a particular place. A man or a woman for example, who embodied this quality, was particularly fit to heal, lead or govern. The occupying Romans tended to reify these pantheistic, ancestral and tribal presences into local Gods or Goddesses. They identified them with their own, quite different, theistic deities – a practice only resisted by the Celtic fringes.[21]

Research into the Celtic tradition allowed me to understand the full significance of Avalon as the location in time and space of the portal for the soul journeying between the worlds. I understood how this significance accounted for the myths and qualities attributed to the Glastonbury Avalon, and how the awareness of the portal for the soul on its journey between the worlds resonated on long after the Celtic period. I summarise these features in the accompanying box.

Glastonbury Traditions of Avalon

- Glastonbury has all the attributes of the Celtic Otherworld: it was an island, surrounded by a plain, near the sea, lying to the west of most of the cultural area it served, with unusual trees and creatures.
- Glastonbury Tor is the home of Gwynn, son of Nudd, an underworld and riverine deity honoured in the area. Gwynn, 'white one' is a leader of the fairy folk and a psychopomp, a guide between the worlds. He rides out at Samhain, with the Wild Hunt, to gather up the souls of the dead.

- The Tor is the abode of a local variant of Gwynn – Melwas, King of the Summerland, from which comes Somerset. The 'Summerland' is another name for the Celtic Otherworld. In northern Britain, Gwynn is identified with Arthur.
- A solar goddess, a primary life source, resided upon the Tor – to and from whom were escorted the living and the dead.
- Gwynn and the Wild Hunt are assisted in their work by the 'Punkies', the guiding lights of the marsh fairy folk.
- Dod Lane, the 'road of the dead', runs between the Abbey and the Tor. Indeed, the Abbey is sited upon this ancient road.
- Local tradition says another road of the dead, 'Arthur's Hunting Path', runs from Cadbury Castle to the Tor. Prehistoric burials near Cadbury are aligned to the Tor and one is provided with a boat.
- The dead were taken into the fairy realm and offered food. Glastonbury is described as 'hungry for the death of pagans'.
- The Tor is said to be hollow. It possesses a cave, the entrance to the underworld.
- King Arthur was taken to Avalon to heal from his wounds. There he sleeps, and will awaken in the hour of greatest need. The Arthurian literature says he was to be healed by Morgen le Fay, whose home is Glastonbury.
- The fairy folk, including Gwynn, needed banishment from the Tor upon the arrival of Christianity. St. Collen met Gwynn and conducted an exorcism on the Tor.
- Glastonbury features the apple tree as the food favoured by those at the Immortal Feast. Avalon = *aballon*, 'apple' in Welsh.
- Glastonbury possessed a church, not built, it is said, by the hands of men, 'but by God himself ... consecrated to Himself and to Holy Mary, Mother of God'.
- Joseph of Arimathea buried two cruets containing the 'blood and sweat of the prophet Jesus' (and the cup used at the Last Supper) near the Chalice Well. 'From that day forth', the legends say, 'the waters of the spring flowed red with the healing blood of Christ'.
- As attested by such strange and diverse sources as John Dee, Abbot Dunstan and the early British seer Melkin, Glastonbury was the source of the 'red and white powders', the 'Mercury of the Philosophers', the 'Universal Solvent', the 'Red and White Elixirs' of the alchemists, capable of achieving the highest initiation of them all – soul transmutation.

CHRISTIAN AVALON

Understanding Glastonbury as the Celtic gateway between the worlds provided me with the key to understanding the Christian traditions of Glastonbury. The legends of the visit by Christ, of the visit by Joseph of Arimathea, of the burial of the two cruets and the Holy Grail, of the exorcism of the Tor by St. Collen,[22] of the miracle of the Holy Thorn tree, of the early dedication to St. Mary, of Morgen le Fay and the burial of King Arthur, make perfect sense in a context where the monks of the Abbey lived in the surviving aura and lingering folklore of Glastonbury as a, if not the, Celtic Avalon.

In the Celtic world, all departing souls made the passage through the portal of Avalon, and the soul who went through and came back after three days to become the saviour of the Christian world, naturally would have made the journey through such an important portal as Glastonbury. Hence the legend of Christ coming to Glastonbury and the tradition of the first church being built by him. The most reliable source of this tradition is William of Malmesbury. He wrote c. 1135 CE that in western Britain was 'a certain royal island, called by the ancient speech Glastonia ... dedicated to the most sacred of deities ... (where there is a) church not built by the art of men ... but by God himself ... consecrated to Himself and to Holy Mary, Mother of God'.[23]

Celtic mythology provides many descriptions of the dead returning to life after immersion in a cauldron. Such a transformative symbol as a cauldron was indubitably part of the pre-Christian mythos of Avalon and it made perfect sense for the equivalent symbol in the Christian tradition, the Holy Grail or cup used by Christ at the last supper, to be brought and buried here. Joseph of Arimathea was associated with this cup; although the texts – trying to make sense of other potentially conflicting stories – have him bring only the two cruets containing the blood and sweat from Christ's wounds.[24] It is the later Arthurian legends that firmly locate the Grail in Glastonbury. The symbols of the Grail legends congregate around the all-compelling power of Avalon. Arthur's seat, the infamous Camelot for example, is now at Cadbury Castle, in plain view of the Tor. Arthur's sword and symbol of sovereignty, Excalibur, say the legends, was forged upon the Isle of Avalon and was returned there from Pomparles Bridge. The Fisher King's Castle, so important in the Arthurian legend of Perceval, now rests on

St. Collen and Gwynn ap Nudd

One day St. Collen, ex-abbot of Glastonbury, having taken up a hermitage beside a spring at the foot of the Tor, overheard two peasants talking about the castle of Gwynn ap Nudd concealed within the Tor. The King of Faery held court there, and welcomed folk to it, but strange things would occur. A person could enter the castle for what they thought was a night and a day and not return for many years, if they returned at all.

The saint said such talk was the work of the Devil. The men warned Collen that lesser things than this upset Gwynn and he might have to answer for it.

Sure enough that evening a messenger appeared at Collen's door. He was human but not quite human. He carried an invitation from Gwynn for the saint to visit the castle. The saint refused. The invitation came the next day and the saint refused again. But when the invitation came for the third time Collen knew he had to go. He filled a phial with holy water and he made his way up the Tor.

He was led into the shining castle of Gwynn ap Nudd. It was the fairest castle he had ever seen. It had the best appointed hosts and many musicians with every kind of music. It had horses with boys on their backs, the fairest in the world, and girls of noble aspect, lively activity, light footed, lightly dressed, in the flower of young age. It had every dignity that was known to the court of a powerful king. Collen was taken into a great hall where a feast was in progress, music played and the finely dressed fairy folk enjoyed themselves. All the fairies wore red and white, the livery of Annwn.

At the end of the great hall Gwynn sat on a golden throne. He greeted St. Collen cordially, asking him if he would eat. But the saint knew the danger of eating fairy food and so declined, saying, 'I do not eat the leaves of a tree!'

Gwynn grew angry and asked, 'What is the matter? Have you not seen such fine food before? Have you not seen folk clad in such finely coloured clothes?'

To this Collen replied, 'Although the food and the manner of dressing is very fine, red is the colour of fire and white is the colour of frost and cold'. He then took out the phial of holy water and scattered it all around. Slowly, Gwynn, the fairies and the castle vanished into the mists. Finally there was only the Saint, the wind and tumps of grass on the lonely Tor top.

Wearyall Hill, the sign of Pisces in the Glastonbury Zodiac. And the great vision of Arthur when he saw the 'glorious Mother of the Lord, bearing her Son in her arms' and was given a crystal cross, took place at the chapel at Beckery beside Wearyall Hill.[25] The final act of mythical congruency is, of course, the finding of the body of Arthur in the Abbey grounds. This is described in a moment.

The cauldron is a feminine symbol of rebirth, sovereignty and inspiration in the Celtic tradition. The practices that honoured the divine feminine in Avalon during the time of the Celts easily led to the establishment of the cults of St. Mary and St. Brigit in Glastonbury. Hence the dedication of the early church at Beckery to Brigit, the dedication of the 'Old Church' on the Abbey site to St. Mary, and the mythic association of them both through the Arthurian legends to the Grail. The dedication to Brigit is particularly significant as she not only presides over fire but also holy wells, while the Mary/mother dedication in the Abbey is likely to predate all others in Britain by an extremely long period of time.[26] The association with Avalon of Morgen or Morganis, later Morgan le Fay, remembers the vital role of the feminine and the strong roles of women in the pre-Christian customs of Avalon.

It was Celtic practice to place a great tree at its sacred centres, or for these centres themselves to be established within a natural grove. The tree was the World Tree, the axis of the world, connecting all realms through its roots, trunk and branches. The World Tree, the *axis mundi*, the World Mountain, the omphalos, the navel of the world, are all symbols inherent to Avalon as the portal between the worlds. Indeed, the name of Avalon derives from the Welsh for apple, *aballon*. It therefore made sense to the Christians to have the miracle of the Holy Thorn take place here as a symbol of the blossoming of their foundation upon an ancient sacred site. Hence the planting of the staff of Joseph of Arimathea on Wearyall Hill, and the perpetuation of the traditions surrounding the Holy Thorn tree ever since.

The monks of Glastonbury made great capital from 'discovering' the body of Arthur beside the Old Church in the late 12th Century. The story of Arthur being 'taken to Avalon for the healing of his wounds', put about by Geoffrey of Monmouth, is elaborated in his *Life of Merlin* in terms that clearly describe the Celtic Otherworld. The place is called the 'Fortunate Isle', where there is no labour, nor illness of any kind.[27] The story of Arthur is developed by Caradoc of Llancarfan in his *Life of Gildas,* where Avalon is unequivocally treated in terms of the Celtic Otherworld. It is known as the 'summer region', a common Celtic

Alchemy and the Prophecy of Melkin

By the time the mysterious prophecy of Melkin – thought to be the sixth century Welsh bard Maelgwn of Gwynedd – was written down by Abbey historians it was almost incomprehensible. *Insula Avallonis avida funere paganorum, prae ceteris in orbe as sepulturam eorum*, it begins: 'The Isle of Avalon, hungry for the death of pagans above all others in the world...' After describing various objects such as thirteen spheres and many people (104,000) buried there, it closes with, 'when the tomb that holds the two vessels filled with the blood and the sweat of the prophet Jesus ... is found ... neither water nor heavenly dew will be lacking for the inhabitants of the most holy isle'.

The key to Melkin's prophecy lies in the alchemical understanding and description of the soul portal of Avalon. The prophecy describes the pre-eminence of Avalon for the transition and rebirth of souls. The 'Great Work' of alchemy is precisely that of the transmutation and purification of the soul in life and death. This is achieved internally in human nature through the 'Elixir of Eternal Life', and externally in the elements through the 'Philosophers' Stone'. Both depend upon the 'chymical wedding' of the 'Red and the White Powders'. These are the first two substances, the alchemists said, which brought creation out of the *prima materia* of the universe. Some alchemists describe the 'Royal Marriage' of the Red and White Powders as the union of two dragons or 'sperms'.

St. Dunstan was alleged by John Dee to have found the two powders. The suggestion being that the Elixir, which transmutes the soul, and the Stone, which purifies it in life, are present on the Isle of Avalon. The alchemical retort in which this process occurs is the aquifer within the Tor. 'The two vessels filled with the blood and the sweat', are the upper and lower parts of the aquifer that distil the Elixir of 'heavenly dew' for auspicious and purified rebirth; while the Stone is the Tor itself, through which the soul can be transmuted for a beneficial return to the *prima materia* of creation. The Red and White Springs are the waters through whose medium the 'Royal Marriage' takes place. The local and most explicit symbolism of this process are the twin serpents – the 'sperms' of the Caduceus – entwined around Excalibur, the sword forged on the Isle of Avalon.

name for the Otherworld. In fact, Caradoc's account of Avalon is entirely prefigured in the Celtic stories told in the Welsh *Mabinogion*, where it is the scene of an otherworldly and cosmological struggle between Gwynn ap Nudd and his rival.[28] The tradition finally comes home with Giraldus Cambrensis, who provides the account of finding Arthur's body on the '*insula Avalonia*'.[29] Apart from the fact that the monks wanted Arthur's body to be preserved in the Abbey as a profitable relic – and were prepared to go to great lengths to fabricate and embellish the tradition, which therefore has many contradictions – the obvious point here is that everyone felt a figure so fundamental to the native British tradition as Arthur had to pass into its Otherworld through its most conspicuous portal – Avalon. Where, of course, he is not dead, but sleeping. The older Celtic worldview might say his soul – or the aspect of Arthur's soul that manifests the ancestral character and sovereignty of the land of Britain – awaits reincarnation. And not just reincarnation anywhere, but through the portal of Avalon. Where he went in is of course the same place as where he will come out.

ABBEY WATER

From time to time wooden pipes or stone conduits come to light beneath Chilkwell Street. It is thought that the pipes either date from the time when Glastonbury Abbey was flourishing and needed a good and constant water supply or when Glastonbury was enjoying popularity as a spa in the 18th century. Water from Chalice Well still flows below Chilkwell Street into the Abbey grounds and fills the medieval fish ponds there, but it has lost all its red deposit. St. Dunstan, Abbot of Glastonbury in the early 10th century, is generally credited with providing the Abbey with its water supply. A section of the pipeline was found in the earth directly before the buildings that presently comprise Chalice Well. The old and well-worn path that runs before these buildings is on the route for a pipe to run from the Abbey to the spring. So it is easy to imagine walking up this path from Chilkwell Street into the valley at the time of St. Dunstan.

The scene has changed considerably from a thousand years before. The path has a hard surface of cobbles, and there are solid buildings along its route. Down below on the right, there is still provision for the watering of animals, but this now takes the form of well-carved stone troughs. The troughs range in length from three to six feet long and are set in a manner that allows one to overflow into the next.

▲ The Tower of St. Michael on the Tor.

There is the pleasant sound of falling water. A well-maintained path ascends the Tor itself, and between the branches of the trees it is possible to see the outline of several buildings on the summit.

There is a detour from the path up the Tor that goes to the White Spring. This allows visitors and residents of the Monastery of St. Michael on the Tor access to the nearest source of good water. From there they can carry it to the summit. Apart from the usual trough for animals and spouts for the filling of water vessels, there is also a stone shrine. It is set into the hillside above the cave entrance, and although there is no admittance to the casual visitor, it contains a statue of St. Brigit. The shrine is cluttered, there is barely enough room to turn around in, but someone must come daily to keep the sacred flame burning.

The entrance to the cave is sealed. Large stones placed across the entrance check admittance. Its hard to get near the spring as the custodians, in the employ of the Abbey, are obviously instructed not to allow the curious to stir up any sediment which would then flow into the drinking arrangements below. But no one is watching, and it is possible to see that behind the stones lies a low tunnel, supported in places by drystone walling, curving into the hillside. The entrance is thoroughly sealed, however, and the whole thing is surmounted by a cross, and above that the shrine of St. Brigit. She is clearly the protector of this place and the protector from god knows what is sealed up under the Tor. If the visitor can't get in, it is also clear that whatever is in there can't get out. It's all a bit disquieting really; as though the spring gushing from the high hill has of late been the scene of an exorcism.

Away from the troughs, back down in the valley, it is all very quiet as the water is now piped underground. Although yew trees are still here, there is no longer the vivid red gash running between them down the centre of the valley. Everything is very well maintained and orderly, and permission must be obtained from a monk who dwells nearby before proceeding. If he were to speak he would no doubt tell the cost – underwritten by a wealthy local benefactor – of heading the well and piping its waters to the Abbey grounds.

The path narrows but is well surfaced, and the wooden pipes – made from elm, which never rots if kept wet – lie directly beneath it. The trees begin to close in, and the vegetation thickens on the steep banks. There is Enchanter's Nightshade, good for sleeping, Hedge Woundwort, good for wounds, Mare's Tail, good for soap, Dog's Mercury, good for, well, let us pass over that, and the ubiquitous Hart's Tongue Fern. The trees above are oak, yew, ash, holly, hawthorn and, wherever it can find a space, elder.

▲ Conjectural reconstruction of the well house for Chalice Well c.1200 CE. The shaded stones remain in place.

A small trickle appears, where once there was a stream, on the right hand side. Here the redness deposited by the water reappears, but there are no pools of any size, and the algae that was such a feature of the pools in earlier times is regularly cleaned away. A low stone wall lies across the well head. It is made of finely carved blocks and runs from one side of the coombe to the other, a distance of about eight feet on its top course. As each block is two feet in length and a foot in height, it has not taken many to form a heading for the well. Behind the wall is a chamber, covered by a wooden hatch, about three feet square inside and three feet deep, full of bubbling, vibrant water. A small square exit for the water is set at the foot of the bottom course of the exterior wall. This is the outlet that connects directly to the wooden pipe. There is some excess water that seeps out through an overflow and into the old streambed. It is all very red.

There is already a problem with debris coming down the sides of the coombe and it is clear that at some point the walls of the chamber will have to be built up. The present wooden hatch is plainly inadequate to prevent rain and groundwater coming in. Only sealed and elevated walls will solve the problem, while a small vertical door on the front of the chamber, above the present wall, would allow inspection.

This is exactly what happened a few hundred years later. The chamber behind and above the wall was built up to form a square well house with a corbelled roof of dressed stone. The amount of debris filling the valley however has increased to an extraordinary level. The reason for this? Most of the trees in the valley and on the sides of Chalice Hill and the Tor have gone. It is the early 13th century, and workers are clearing all available land for the benefit of the Abbey. The climate is warm and there are even vines running around the terraces on the newly reclaimed hillsides. The clearing of the trees meant erosion, and sediment has washed down the valley to all but fill what was once a deeply incised V-shaped coombe at its base. It is apparent that the well house will soon be entirely below ground. The fill has already reached roof level at the rear of the chamber, and all the springs that once washed the sediment away are tapped and controlled for use by the Abbey.

The well house was never really a freestanding structure. It was originally a chamber inserted in the bottom of a little coombe to tap the spring water that rose there, and was built up as a response to the rapid in-filling of the coombe – due to agriculture – in the 12th and 13th centuries. Although the size and shape of the original structure is known, as it has survived in its lower part and there are other examples in the area, it is hard to know exactly what the roof of the original chamber looked like. It was destroyed at a later time, and it is through the remnants of the roof that visitors now look into the well today.[30]

It is not clear how long the original well house stood before becoming entirely covered by the rising ground. The Abbey must have had some way of gaining access to the system and especially to the underground pipes carrying the water away from the well. The dissolution of the Abbey in the mid sixteenth century was perhaps the turning point in the fortunes of the well house. The system may have fallen into neglect, as the need for the water in the Abbey grounds diminished. Subsequent owners of the Abbey fishponds however kept the water flowing, but probably lacked the resources to do anything but the

▲ The Well House c. 1300 CE. Drawing by Alan Royce.

minimum necessary maintenance. It was this state of affairs that prevailed for the next 200 years when it was again time for construction at the Chalice Well.

EIGHTEENTH CENTURY AVALON

In the 1700s the ruins of the Abbey provided the stone for many houses along the length of Chilkwell Street. Glastonbury was thriving as a small market town, and it was hoped its position on a network of waterways would give it a commercial edge. Bristol and Bath to the north developed enormously during this time and the interest in spas was strong. Although salvation through faith was the primary motivation of pilgrims coming to Glastonbury in an earlier age there was also great interest in healing and miraculous cures and this interest persisted into the eighteenth century. The extraordinary hills and springs are of course still here, the aura from the medieval age lingered on, and as visitors began to testify to healing from drinking the waters of Avalon it was easy for the town to capitalise once more on the theme of miracles.

In the valley, a cluster of buildings proclaims various purposes. One houses a brewery, taking advantage of the copious water supply. Another building has a religious sect interested in it as a chapel. There are farm workers cottages, simple affairs with large fireplaces, whose inhabitants draw water from a stone culvert that runs, mostly uncovered, in the street before them. The house demanding most immediate attention however is the one with many signs offering services to those who have come in search of a cure.

The house, the Anchor Inn as it turns out, offers lodgings of every sort, transportation, subscriptions, bottled water with the label 'Chalice Well', and above all the opportunity to drink and bathe in the 'especial and healing waters' of the place. The healing powers of the water are confirmed by the many written testimonies on display. One crucial testimony by Matthew Chancellor, signed in 1750, claims healing of a long-standing asthmatic condition by the taking of the waters on seven successive Sundays. There is quite a crowd here, reading the various signs, discussing their symptoms, examining the claims and trophies of those who have been cured on the walls and waiting to use the baths.

The yew trees are still here, but the place is considerably cleared and cultivated fields run up the sides of the valley. The ground has risen further, and is levelled for the purposes of the lanes and paths that cross it. Just beyond the first group of yew trees there is a wall with a gate

▲ The Bathhouse at Chalice Well, c. 1753. Drawing by Alan Royce.

barring admission for those who are not patrons of the inn. Beyond the wall is a rectangular building containing baths. The largest bath is surrounded by people soaking limbs or immersing their entire body in the cold water. Smaller baths are for bathing infected parts and there is a fountain with little spouts and attached cups. There is also a private bathhouse set to one side, with facilities to suit the wealthier of the patrons.[32] The flagstones on the floor of the large bathhouse and the slots in them for the pillars that supported the roof on the open west side can still be seen today. It is not exactly on a grand scale; the place has not received investment for very long; but there is a briskness in the air that suggests the proprietor – Ann Gallaway, the 'Bath Mistress General' – is seeking every way she can to develop her opportunity.

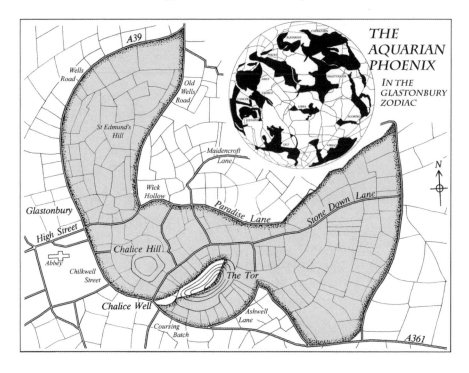

The well head, once a partially above ground medieval well house, is now completely below ground. The only means of access to it is through the cover in the roof. The sides of the old well chamber, now a well shaft, are rebuilt in their upper courses and another chamber added on the southwest side where the original inspection hatch lay. The new chamber plus the old well shaft combine to form a reservoir for the baths. The reservoir fills slowly over the hours of the night to form a head of water that quickly fills the baths during the day. The new chamber is made of courses of ashlar (dressed stone blocks) between courses of baked brick to make it watertight. It is irregular in size and set in the ground according to the bedrock. The roof is a brick vault. It is evident that the new chamber will create enough pressure to send the waters of the well all the way into town where a pumphouse is being planned. It is also evident that another purpose of the structure is to keep out any contamination from other springs or from surface drainage. Cattle and sheep are grazing everywhere and it is a problem keeping the water undisturbed and clean. It is likely that a small structure, probably built of wood, was placed over the well to reduce contamination and prevent unauthorised access. There are many people coming to seek a cure from the healing waters.

The Glastonbury Zodiac

In the late 16th Century, Dr. John Dee, scholar, alchemist, astrologer and physician to Queen Elizabeth I, visited Somerset and recorded what he called 'Merlin's Secret'. He wrote:

> The starres which agree with their reproductions on the ground do lye onlie on the celestial path of the Sonne, moon and planets ... all the greater starres of Sagittarius fall in the hinde quarters of the horse, while Altiar, Tarazes and Alsschain from Auilla do fall on its cheste ... thus is astrologie and astronomie carefullie and exactley married and measured in a scientific reconstruction of the heavens ...

Dee was dismissed as a maverick, until in 1929 an artist, Kathryn Maltwood, published *A Guide to Glastonbury's Temple of the Stars*. While studying the Arthurian legends and with the aid of maps and aerial photographs, she noticed an extraordinary pattern. Inspired by John Dee, she described this pattern as a replica of the stellar signs of the Zodiac upon the ground.

The terrestrial zodiac around Glastonbury is formed by the combination of natural features such as rivers and hills, and man-made features such as field boundaries, mounds and causeways. The figure of Aquarius for example, is formed by the natural hills and boundaries of the Isle of Avalon, and developed by earth banks and roads. The twelve signs of the Zodiac cover an area with a circumference of thirty miles. Some figures are many miles in length. Occasionally a figure differs from the standard pattern; Aquarius, for example, is not the Water Bearer but a bird whose form is made by the whole of the Isle of Avalon. The bird drinking from the White Spring and Chalice Well makes the connection with water. Kathryn Maltwood called the bird the Aquarian Phoenix. The phoenix renews itself through fire, perpetuating the death and rebirth themes of Avalon.

The *Gentlemen's Magazine* reported that on one day alone, Sunday, 5 May 1752, 'above ten thousand people came to Glastonbury ... to drink the waters there for their health'. The roads were congested with their carts and carriages. Lodging was at a premium. Ten thousand people

The Glastonbury Tor Labyrinth

The idea that the terraces on the Tor form a three dimensional labyrinth was first suggested in 1968 by Geoffrey Russell. Geoffrey Ashe subsequently walked and surveyed the labyrinth in 1979. Both claim that a path threads around the terraces according to a classical design found throughout the world. The classical labyrinth appears for example in Spanish, Cornish and Irish rock carvings, as a traditional design motif among the Pima, Tohono O'odham and Hopi tribes of North America, in Javanese and Indian art, in European stone and turf mazes, and on coins and inscriptions from the ancient Mediterranean.

The meanings of the labyrinth include fertility, death and rebirth – the journey and the return from the land of the dead. For the Tohono O'odham, of Arizona for example, the labyrinth represents the path around the sacred mountain of Baboquivari. The path was made so the living could not follow the dead into the spirit world. For the Hopi, the labyrinth is a symbol of emerging spirit as well as the child in the womb. The labyrinth of King Minos of Crete was the scene of death for those imprisoned within it. European stone and turf labyrinths are places of prayer, of weather magic, and of races to catch and kiss maidens. The labyrinth on the Tor however is many times larger than those made upon the ground, and it possesses, like the sacred mountain of Baboquivari, a vertical dimension.

Although probably beginning life as an 'academic invention', the classical labyrinth design for the Tor utilizes most of the higher terraces and works well due to the pear-shape of the Tor providing a single axis and ascent way. Other hill shapes make it difficult for the labyrinth design to work. There are problems however with the design that means the terraces were not originally carved to be a labyrinth. The terraces are an amalgamation of events over the years. The 'Druid Stones' on the southwest ascent route mark key points in the labyrinth. The lower one, the 'Living Rock', marks the entrance. Walking the labyrinth one way can take some time, and is advisable only on a dry day.

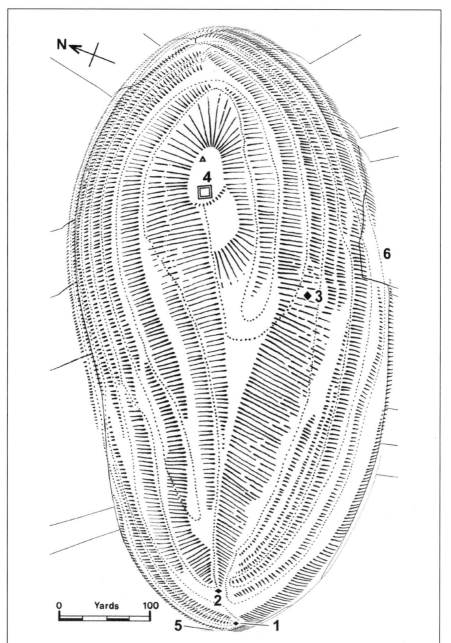

▲ **Tor Labyrinth.** Key: 1. The first Druid Stone, the 'Living Rock'. 2.
The second Druid Stone. 3. Eggstone. 4. St. Michael's Tower. 5. Entrance
to Labyrinth. 6. Present day field boundaries.

on one day does not seem to be much of an exaggeration, as records exist of numerous cures and by 1753, 'a pump-room, baths and other conveniences' were built at Chain Gate in Magdalene Street.[33] In June of 1752, the *Gloucester Journal* contained an advertisement, evidently placed by Ann Gallaway, that encouraged subscriptions and season tickets, offered lodgings and reported the construction of 'a commodious house, pump-house and baths'. It also provided a list of cures, ranging from leprosy, asthma, dropsy and rheumatic pains to the 'king's evil' and 'scorbutic disorders'. The practice of taking the waters for seven successive Sundays, after the original healing of Matthew Chancellor, continued. An eye witness – who went on to collect numerous testimonies – wrote: 'I found a vast Number of people in various Conditions; of whom, some told me they were cured, but would nevertheless tarry the Seven Sundays, which is the usual Way there; and others who were much better, and waiting in Hope of being perfectly well'.[34] Despite this popularity, Glastonbury only enjoyed about ten years as a spa. After the death of a visitor, either because the water was polluted or because too much was drunk in search for a cure, people went to take the more copious and far warmer waters of Bath. The pumphouse can still be seen in Magdalene Street and across the road the waters of the well emerge from a pipe after filling the Abbey fishponds.

There remains one important description of the healing spa in Glastonbury a few decades after its decline. *Phelps' Magazine* for Somerset reported in 1836 that the 'far-famed and wonder-working water rises at the western foot of the Tor Hill, near the Anchor Inn. Its source is under a high bank, and is carried by a pipe across the road.... There is another mineral spring which ... is strongly chalybeate'. This makes it clear that both the waters of the White Spring and the Red Spring were taken into the baths and used for healing. There are no records from the 1750s that distinguish between the two springs and say that one was good for one cure and one for another, or that both should be used in sequence, or as a mix and in what parts. Yet it is entirely likely that such practices sprung up among the patrons of the spa, based on the experiences of those reporting cures around them.

TWENTIETH CENTURY AVALON

As I became aware of how the energetic qualities of the Tor gave rise to the many Avalonian traditions, it became possible to understand what has taken place here in more recent times. The many traditions: the Celtic

▲ The 'Living Rock' on the southwest ascent route marks the entrance into the Labyrinth.

pagan, the Christian, the Arthurian, the 18th century healing traditions and so on, can be understood in the light of the extraordinary geophysical properties of the Tor. In turn, they influence each other and this rich mix forms the basis for the present.

The Glastonbury Zodiac is a case in point: it provides an example of a universal symbol being attracted to and emerging from the qualities and traditions of Avalon. The eleven mile wide imprint of the zodiacal pattern of stars upon the local landscape demonstrates the alchemical adage, 'as above, so below'. A place which possesses a world mountain, a world axis – which global traditions say has Polaris fixed to its summit and has the stars revolving about it – inevitably finds a way to manifest the heavenly dimension upon its terrestrial domain. As there is no greater symbol of the transcendent 'other' world than the heavens, it is easy to maintain from this, the terrestrial dimension, that the home of the soul is among the stars. The attribution of the landscape Zodiac to Avalon is because the zodiac of stars suggests a pattern for life far greater than that of this world and as the greater pattern for life lies in the realm of the soul, so the place where the soul makes its entrance and exit in this world naturally becomes the place of the stars.

The Pulling Power of Avalon Today

In the 12th century text, the *Life of Merlin*, the author (possibly Geoffrey of Monmouth) puts into the mouth of the Celtic bard Taliesin, a description of 'the Isle of Apples'. Taliesin says that nine sisters rule this Fortunate Isle and of them the eldest, Morgen, is the most skilful. The wounded Arthur is placed under her care. Here the author is drawing on an earlier Welsh text, *Preiddeu Anwnn*, attributed to the 6th Century Taliesin, which says the 'cauldron of the Lord of Annwn' (Annwn is the Celtic Otherworld) is in the keeping of nine women. Arthur attempts to gain the cauldron, but the journey to Annwn is extremely perilous and all but seven of his company die in the attempt.

These texts demonstrate the ability of the Isle of Avalon to draw in themes from Celtic, Classical and Arthurian mythology in its great period as the 'Motherchurch' of Britain. But this is not all. The role of the mythic themes, symbols and characters described in murky texts like the *Life of Merlin* continue to be developed by those in the neo-pagan and Goddess inspired movements in Avalon today. In the books of Kathy Jones for example, Morgen becomes a 'Ninefold Sisterhood of the Morgens'. They operate as muses, healers and seers, while Morgen herself 'helps those who are dying to cross over to the Other Side of life'. The Celtic cauldron, the Christian Grail and the role of Otherworld guide are claimed for the priestesses of Avalon, who 'lived and served the Lady'.

The gateway between the worlds, the *axis mundi* of the Tor, has the ability to draw in and elaborate upon the universal imagery and symbolism of the Otherworld. It is a living temple, and will attract many traditions and practices to itself. It claims the site of the first Christian church. It has attracted the legends of the Grail and the traditions of alchemy. It has attracted the appellation of *shambhala* – the equivalent of Avalon from the central Asian tradition. It has attracted the labyrinth, the symbol of the pathway between the worlds. It has drawn to itself the vesica piscis, the Zodiac, the Temple of the Stars, and now it features the 'first Goddess Temple in the British Isles for 1600 years'. Only the passage of time will reveal what is next drawn by the pull of its compelling otherworldly power.

As the many traditions of the world become known in the modern age, the symbols within them that possess universal meaning rapidly transplant themselves across the globe to fitting locations. The Glastonbury Tor labyrinth – like the Glastonbury Zodiac – is another instance of a global sacred symbol taking up home in a place of appropriate tradition. The labyrinth, a universal symbol of the path of the soul to and from the Otherworld, now exists in the location where the gateway between the worlds has long been revered.

Although the terraces of the Tor cannot be shown to be deliberately carved to form a labyrinth, and were embellished in the Christian era to fashion a seven-tiered Calvary Mount, the symbolic meanings add up to the same thing. The Calvary Mount signifies the journey undertaken by Christ on his journey to death, while the labyrinth is the pathway to the Otherworld. In the Christian tradition, as in many traditions, the World Mountain has seven levels and the path to the Otherworld passes through seven layers. 'This land of Utmost Happiness', says the Buddhist *Amitabha Sutra*, 'is surrounded by seven tiers of embankments, by seven layers of veils, and by seven rows of trees'. The pagan classical labyrinth with its seven concentric paths, the Christian Calvary Mount with its seven tiers and seven Stations of the Cross, the Buddhist Pure Land with its various sevenfold features, all find complete congruence upon Glastonbury Tor. The pedantic might point out there are over twenty terraces upon the Tor, but to the eye from most elevations, seven is the number most frequently seen. The archpedantic might point out that the majority of the terraces in the form they exist today are agricultural lynchets, and this is also true; but nevertheless the labyrinth exists and will continue to develop as more people thread its sinuous course.

As well as the Calvary Mount upon the Tor, many other universal symbols were added to the Avalonian iconography in the Christian period. Adoration of the original Holy Thorn tree on Wearyall Hill for example became so great that an iconoclastic puritan cut it down. While this suggests on the one hand that there was fundamentally too great a division between the Christian gospels and the imagery of the World Tree at the centre of life, on the other hand it reveals that the Church – at least in its early stages – deliberately sought to align itself to the ancient and universal symbols. At the same time, although the position of the 'Old Church' in the Abbey grounds appears to be one of the few locations on Avalon where the Tor cannot be seen, in fact it is placed exactly on the alignment of the rising sun over the Tor and Chalice Hill. The precise positioning of the 'Motherchurch' of Britain upon ancient patterns shows the Church was keenly aware of the properties of the Tor as a cosmic and world centre.[35] The subsequent attempts on the part of the Abbey to bring not only King Arthur but his queen, his court and the whole entourage of ancient symbolic talismans – including the Holy Grail, the descendant of the Celtic cauldrons of rebirth, inspiration and plenty – to Avalon, show how important it was to the Church to achieve mythical congruency with its foundation.

Given this practice of 'mythical congruency' in the past, it comes as no surprise to find that it continues in Glastonbury today. People continue to draw upon and reshape the ancient traditions to help them understand, legitimise and give authority to their experience of the energy of Avalon. Glastonbury is enjoying immense popularity as a place of spiritual renaissance and this modern role began around the beginning of the twentieth century. Wellesley Tudor Pole brought his 'Holy Grail' to Glastonbury with the find of the blue bowl at Beckery in 1904. This inspired Alice Buckton to pioneer the revival of Chalice Well from 1913 (described below), a mission finally completed by Tudor Pole in 1958. Frederick Bligh Bond drew attention to the sacred geometry of the Abbey as well as the use of psychometry with his experiments in automatic writing. The vesica piscis designed by Bligh Bond after the Great War as a cover for the Chalice Well is a fine example of the energy of Avalon drawing a universal symbol to itself. As described in the section on Chalice Well, the portal revealed in the eternal procession of the ratios and forms of the vesica piscis makes it the ideal symbol of Chalice Well and of Avalon as a whole.

Between the wars, Rutland Boughton drew attention to pagan mythic traditions in his operas and Dion Fortune contributed greatly to the revival of occult tradition. She was followed by Geoffrey Ashe after the war – both dwelling in the same property upon the slopes of the Tor. In the 1930s Kathryn Maltwood developed landscape geomancy on a hitherto undreamt of scale with her Glastonbury Zodiac, and this subject was taken up and developed by Mary Caine in the 1960s. In the 1970s John Michell drew attention to the vast 'St. Michael Line' passing through the axis of Glastonbury Tor and ley lines have fuelled many a debate ever since. The list of luminaries, free thinkers and spiritual revolutionaries associated with Glastonbury in recent years goes on and on. They all built on the basis of Avalon being the pathway of the soul between this world and the next. There is no other reason, no other explanation for this otherwise small and quite ordinary Somerset town to occupy the position it does as a centre of global spiritual significance.

THE TOR AND VALLEY TODAY

Most notable among the recent acts that have taken place on or beside the Tor are the building of the reservoir for the waters of the White Spring in 1872 and the occupancy of the Chalice Well property by Alice Buckton from 1913 to her death in 1944. The first was a profane act that caused the ancient significance of the White Spring to become quite lost, while the second was entirely different. The presence of Alice Buckton allowed the spiritual significance of Chalice Well to resume and flourish.

After the brief period of time in the 18th century when the valley and its springs became a spa, the inn maintained a commercial presence on the site. First known as the Anchor Inn for reasons not entirely clear, it became Tor House in the early 19th century. Although this building had an attractive Georgian façade it was a jumble at the rear, retaining some features of the earlier inn, including the animal byres. Tor House must have belonged to a fairly wealthy family at some point, for there is a photo circa 1860 of the female members of the family posing outside the house in huge black dresses. The property was acquired shortly after this by a Roman Catholic Order based in Belgium, who turned it into a seminary. The Order made Tor House the headmaster's house, and built a formidable four-storey school building on the junction of Well House Lane and Chilkwell Street. I know very little about the motives of the Order, why they chose Glastonbury or Chalice Well, but they were not on the site for very long before financial difficulties made them give up.

Alice Buckton was drawn to Glastonbury after meeting Wellesley Tudor Pole in 1907. She heard from him the story of the blue bowl, found in Bride's Well, which many at the time believed to be the Holy Grail or at least the cup used by Christ at the last supper. The story of this remarkable object, how it got to be in the sluice known as Bride's Well and what it inspired, is found in Patrick Benham's book, *The Avalonians.* Tudor Pole's books provide accounts of its significance. In 1912 Alice Buckton acquired the Well. She was a talented teacher and writer with a warm nature, who wished to further the education of children and the cause of women. She held a universal metaphysical view, 'the one in the many', and taught self-realisation, especially through the creative arts. She felt at home with the mystical circle around Tudor Pole – and others who were drawn to Glastonbury at this time – especially because of their emphasis on the restoration of the feminine to spirituality. She wished to establish a festival centre in Glastonbury, and put on many plays at Chalice Well, the most famous being *Eager Heart*. She also tried to establish a college for women at the Well, having success with arts and crafts. Dion Fortune, who moved in over the road in 1924, described the traditional methods used for making pottery, for spinning wool and the heavy skeins of dyed wool hung around the orchard to dry. The gardeners at the Well frequently turn up fragments of pottery from the craft workshops of Alice Buckton's era.

It was the goal of Alice Buckton to preserve 'this mother-centre', as a place of spirit and of the dramatic arts into the future. Through her will, made in 1943, she formed Chalice Well Trust. Her goal was the establishment of an 'international and educational service', that worked 'silently as well as explicitly . . . for the healing of the nations'. The place was to be 'interdenominational', a scene of festivals and the arts, and the source of 'refreshment for men and women of goodwill and of every nationality'.[36] Lack of money prevented the realisation of this dream and for a while Chalice Well slipped back into the hands of a school. The goals of the Trust however were realised with the return of Wellesley Tudor Pole, and under his leadership and with his financial support and expertise, the property was secured in 1958.

In 1959 the Chalice Well Trust was formally reinstated. As Alice Buckton originally nominated two of the trustees, and as it was Wellesley Tudor Pole who had originally inspired Alice Buckton, the new Trust formed a continuation of her work. The charter of Chalice Well Trust carried on her wishes: the preservation of the Well, its openness to the public, and the promotion of events – especially the dramatic arts.

The Trust bought land and property adjacent to the Chalice Well. This included a section of the old Fair Field by Chalice Orchard on the other side of Well House Lane. They developed the well, made its waters safe from contamination and landscaped the gardens. The old Catholic seminary building was by now in an awful state and was demolished. Tor House was also removed. The Trust did not have permission to demolish this listed building, but it must have been in poor condition, for when the contractor's demolition ball 'accidentally' struck Tor House it became unstable and had to be removed. Until the mid 1970s the lower part of the gardens was a building site as the demolition and rebuilding work was carried out. The row of cottages beside the old lane to the well was retained, and these form the nucleus of buildings that serve the Trust. The largest cottage, Little St. Michaels, which in Alice Buckton's day was a retreat house for guests, continues to serve in this manner. A sanctuary was built on the top floor according to the design of Wellesley Tudor Pole.

This sanctuary, known as 'The Upper Room', was probably Tudor Pole's primary motivation for securing and developing the property. Ever since the mysterious cup, the 'sapphire' or blue glass bowl, had come into his possession he had sought an appropriate home for it; and now, over fifty years later, he felt this goal was going to be achieved. Tudor Pole kept his metaphysical life quite apart from his business and home life, and here, in his inner world, he was a psychic, a clairvoyant, a spiritual pilgrim – the founder of the silent minute in World War Two – and a believer in visions that had begun for him extremely early in life and led him to his Holy Grail. He believed that through the mediumship of the blue bowl an energy, a transforming influence on a par with the coming of Christ, would return to earth and redeem the struggling nations and people of the world with its presence. Chalice Well was the perfect home for his mystically charged bowl, and after Tudor Pole's death in 1968 it came to permanently reside there. Another 'mythically congruent' symbol had come home.

Aware of their responsibilities to the traditions of Glastonbury and as guardians of much of the little valley in which lies Chalice Well, the current Trustees are determined not to succumb to the commercial interests that have harmed the White Spring. Here, the Water Board and the Town Council, oblivious to their responsibility to return the spring to the public, allowed a local businessman to purchase the spring in the early 1980s.[37] The owner leases out a café in the unsuitable conditions of the dark and dank reservoir and sells the spring water, which after treatment carries few of the qualities of the original water rising under the Tor. Under these circumstances I have heard the opinion expressed that the best approach is to appeal to the owner to become aware of his responsibilities to the extraordinary location and town of which he is a part. If, for example, he were to donate the White Spring to the people of Glastonbury such a gesture would no doubt allow his generosity to be recorded for posterity. It could then be decided whether the interests of the place were best served by becoming part of a trust: whether the National Trust, the Chalice Well Trust, or some other impartial and protective body.

The Water

The Red Spring water that pours out of the Lion's Head in Chalice Well gardens, or from the outlet in Well House Lane, comes directly from its underground source. This is the first occasion the water is exposed to light and air after its lengthy journey through the lower parts of the aquifer below the Tor. The White Spring water is exposed to air in the tunnels and caverns in the upper part of the aquifer, so it is in a relatively different condition when it arrives at the reservoir in Well House Lane.

Upon exposure to the environment on the earth's surface the quality of the water immediately begins to change. The ionic charge of the atoms of the water alters in the presence of the light and air of the atmosphere. The iron in the water oxidises and rapidly precipitates, coating everything it touches with a red deposit. The water is sensitised to and encouraged to pick up the electrical and magnetic forces of the prevailing atmospheric conditions by passing through vortical channels, waterfalls, open pools and flowforms. It becomes warmer, its ions discharge, its atoms lose and gain electrons, it becomes oxygenated, it loses its minerals and accumulates other properties. By the time it reaches the bottom of the Chalice Well garden the character of the water has altered considerably, if not completely. Only immediately above the well and at the Lion's Head can the properties of the water be experienced in its original form.

To preserve the original character of the water, the following procedures are recommended. Gather the water directly from the outlet. Keep the water in an air tight, lightproof container as close as possible to the original temperature of 11 °C, 55 °F. Colder is better than hotter, so keep the water in a fridge. If the container is transparent then do not expose it to sunlight. Keep it as still as possible. If it is impossible to preserve these conditions then the following practice is suggested to restore the water to its original state.

Pour the water into a glass container, or pour some drops of the water into a vessel containing pure water from another source. Stir the water with a neutral instrument, not metal, or rotate it in the hands to create a vortex formation. This allows the greatest inter-action between the molecules of water and the environmental energy. While stirring, meditate upon the original qualities of the water before it emerges from under the Tor. Visualise or evoke in some way whatever it is that represents these original qualities. It may be a prayer, an image – e.g. a photograph of Chalice Well – a feeling, the memory of birdsong on the occasion the water was collected, or the deva, elemental or presence of the deity that embodies this power. Imagine these qualities suffusing the water in the glass container. Although this may not sound like hard science, there is increasing evidence that this method will restore the original potency of the water. This evidence is described in the next section.

ENDNOTES

1. G. Wright, 1870, p. 21.

2. G. Wright, 1894, p. 37.

3. I was unable to find St. Dunstan's Well beside the site of the chapel of the same name (just south of the road to Shepton Mallet past the junction with Ashwell Lane). Local residents told me a well in the area was filled in as it was dangerous.

4. The water for Glastonbury from West Compton was originally pumped into the open reservoir at Ashwell, from there it was pumped to the town and to the tank on the Tor. After 1961 the water was pumped directly to the Tor and to other covered reservoirs (i.e. upper Well House Lane). The pumphouse is on the corner of Chilkwell Street and Cinnamon Lane. The Ashwell reservoir is maintained by the Ashwell Spring, but does no more than keep alive the fish within it.

5. In conversation with local hydrologist and geologist Paul Hodge, I learnt that a large amount of previously 'missing' Mendip water was found rising as fresh water springs on the floor of the Bristol Channel. Due to the geology, Paul was of the opinion that the waters rising in the springs around the Tor were of a local, not a distant origin. See also Peter Hardy, 1999, p. 197.

6. *Presidential Address to Section C*, British Association, 1930. Quoted from F. Welch and R. Crookall, 1935.

7. Philip Rahtz, in 1993 (p. 18), suggested an artesian iron-bearing spring once emerged on or above the present summit of the Tor. The water hardened the Midford Sand, which on erosion could no longer support the spring, so the spring dropped to the point where it emerges today. Philip and I agree on the iron hardened Tor assuming its shape after erosion, but whereas his source of iron-bearing water is from below, my source is from the now vanished strata above.

8. All similar springs in the area have a ground temperature of 10–11 °C.

9. Andrew Portman, during his residency in the old pumphouse, measured the rate of flow of the White Spring over the course of several years; while the staff of Chalice Well – especially Martin Faulkner, then grounds manager of Chalice Well – obtained accurate measurements of that spring over the course of 2002–03. I am extremely grateful for their efforts.

10. There is a spring at Wick that flows at a maximum of 100,000 gpd and a minimum of 8,000 gpd. It reveals traces of iron. It is supplied by the catchment area of Stonedown and so does not affect the figures for the area calculated around the Tor. It does provide further evidence for underlying iron-impregnated strata. Of more relevance is the spring on the far side of the Tor at Ashwell that can flow up to 100,000 gpd. It lies at a higher elevation to the White Spring. It contains no trace of iron. It is subject to rainfall and 'dries up to a trickle' according to local residents in the summer. It drains surface water from the east side of the Tor plus the part of Stonedown adjacent to Ashwell Lane into the open reservoir at Ashwell Farm. See L. Richardson, 1928.

11. From the Chalice Well Archive collection.

12. For more on local geology and springs see *Wells and Springs of Somerset*, L. Richardson. Devonian: Old Red Sandstone at the core of the Mendips, 400–360 million years ago (mya). Carboniferous: limestones deposited under sea, 360–290 mya. Through the Permian and Triassic, 290–208 mya marlstones deposited as area lifts out of sea and folds. Jurassic 208–146 mya, Blue Lias laid down as area under sea again. Cretaceous 146–65 mya Midford Sandstone and overlying deposits laid down. Tertiary and Quaternary 65 mya to present: area uplifted and top layers eroded until oldest structures are revealed.

13. See C. and N. Hollinrake, *An Archaeological Watching Brief at Chalice Well*, 1997, GCW 99, Report Number 145. (Bronze Age radiocarbon date confirmed later.)

14. For an account of Somerset in the Celtic–Roman period see Peter Leach, 2001.

15. Map reference ST 62302520. Robert Tabor, 1999, 'South Cadbury: Milsoms Corner', *Current Archaeology* **163**, pp. 251–255.

16. See J. Armitage Robinson, 1926, p. 1.

17. Philip Rahtz, 1964, pp. 156–157. The yew is preserved in the archives of Chalice Well.

18. *Cormac's Glossary*, Whitley Stokes, Irish Archaeological and Celtic Society, 1868.

19. From the *Song of Amergin*. Translation drawn from the *Leabhar Gabhála*, the 'Book of Invasions'.

20. From *Imram Brain maic Febail*, the 'Voyage of Bran'. Kuno Meyer 1895, Lady Gregory 1904.

21. For a full examination of these tenets see *Druid Magic*, Sutton and Mann, 2000.

22. See S. Baring-Gould and J. Fisher, 'Life of St. Collen', *Lives of the British Saints*, 4 volumes, London, 1907–13, and Charles Squire, *Celtic Myth and Legend*, London, 1905.

23. Trans. F. Lomax, 1992, p. 5 ff. William goes on to describe the first church being built of rushes, and the tradition of there being 'twelve anchorites' or companions forming the company of the island.

24. See, for example, J. Armitage Robinson, 1926, pp. 37–39.

25. Ibid., pp. 20–23. Also James P. Carley, *John of Glastonbury's 'Chronica'*, Oxford, 1978, 77 ff., and in P. Rahtz and S. Hirst, 1974 (includes excavation report of Beckery). The crystal cross was given to Glastonbury Abbey.

26. Geoffrey Ashe 1982, pp. 143–44.

27. Geoffrey of Monmouth, *History*, XI, 2.

28. Caradoc of Llancarfan, *Vita Gildae. Mabinogion* pp. 148, 159, 168.

29. Giraldus Cambrensis, *The Historical Works*.

30. As far as I know, the excavator's case for the square shaft of Chalice Well dating to c. 1200 CE is based upon an inspection made by C. A. R. Radford and A. R. Dufty in February 1960. Report filed in the archives of Chalice Well. See P. Rahtz, 1996, pp. 106–111.

31. P. Rahtz, 1971.

32. In 1870, George Wright describes seeing the footings of these buildings. They were in the area where Arthur's court is today and are clearly marked on the 1844 tithe map.

33. Quoted from G. Wright, ibid., pp. 29–34.

34. Benjamin Matthews, 1751, p. 1.

35. The precise position of the first church in the Abbey grounds is determined by three main factors: the intersection of Dod Lane (the pre-Christian road of the dead) with the alignment of the summit of the Tor over Chalice Hill and the presence of St. Joseph's Well. See Mann, 2001, pp. 81–85. As described in the section on the alignments, it also lies on the solstice 'Dragon Line' between the Mound/Maesbury and Wearyall Hill/Aller.

36. Quoted from a letter by Alice Buckton; given in full in *The Avalonians*, pp. 166–167.

37. It is unfortunate for the reputation of the Town Council that the businessman was a Mason and a Councillor with planning responsibilities at the time, as the closed sale, low price and granting of permits have led to regrettable allegations of insider trading.

PART THREE

THE AVALONIAN
SOUL PORTAL

TOR VORTEX

As a central axis surrounded by the revolving earth and sky, the Tor is a funnel reaching from the point of its summit to a wide base upon the Isle of Avalon below. It also has an entry or ascent route that I will describe in a moment. This funnel, or cone, is not surprising as it was a downward spiralling current of water that formed the Tor in the first place. The image is that of a conical vortex spiralling outwards and downwards in ever widening circles, or rising inward and upward to a point of focus. A spiral vortex is the form employed by nature as the vehicle for its energy, while a spherical vortex is the form employed by the universe for the form of its elementary particles. Science is discovering that a particle of matter is not a solid, but a spinning – and thus inherently stable – 'string' or vortex of energy. Such energy vortices have apparent edges, but their energy extends outwards in fields that fill and are in fact responsible for space. Their 'edges' are merely impressions created by the interaction between them and their observer.[1] The spiral vortex is the form preferred by water – and by other elemental matter in the biological world such as the genetic encoding in DNA – as it creates multiple layers that allow the greatest interaction between the energy vortices that form particles as they pass each other by. The dissolving of sugar or salt crystals in a glass of water upon stirring provides a perfect illustration of this interaction.

The point of focus upon the summit of the Tor is the point of connection with and energy input from the heavenly dimension. Mythology says the summit of the World Mountain, the *axis mundi*, is not only attached to the Pole Star but it also receives lightning from the Gods. Dion Fortune, who lived at its foot, so she should know, felt places such as the Tor were always sacred to the sun. To her, and other mystics at the time, the sun was the source of energy that created life on earth. What is being expressed here – and now it is possible to put it in more scientific terms – is the knowledge that water as the basis for life on earth is at its most receptive to fields of energy, such as the magnetic and electromagnetic fields of the sun, when it moves in a vortex motion. The sun has a great influence upon the electromagnetic fields of the earth and thus upon water. For example, water develops high levels of ionisation while in a rapidly moving vortex and even generates a detectable electrical charge when moving slowly through the tiny threadlike veins of a typical subterranean aquifer. High ionisation

▲ Tor from North

means that the molecules of water are loosely bonded together and the vortices that form their electrons are in a state of flux. In this condition water is able to maintain its purity, develop and enhance life, and receive, dissolve, transform and transmit the nature of other substances and their electromagnetic charges as it comes into contact with them. The Tor, through the combined properties of its elevated aquifer, acts as a generator and a receiver for the pulse of life in the cosmos.

It is also possible to conceive of a funnel descending from the heavens, or ascending from the summit, in a mirror image of the conical Tor. In the same manner as the earth receives and mediates the concentrated energies of the sky through the properties of the Tor, so the sky above receives the energies transmitted from the terrestrial dimension below. Each shapes and reciprocates the other. The image is that of a double vortex somewhat like an egg timer, or, more poetically, like a descending and ascending dragon.

I was struggling to understand and put into words a better description of this energy system until various books about quantum theory, water and the work of Viktor Schauberger came into my hands. Schauberger demonstrated that energy in the natural world flows in vortex patterns of rotation and counter rotation with points of change and equilibrium in-between.[2] Currents of wind and water provide excellent examples of this, but it is also observed in matter on an astrophysical scale. Schauberger believed that water flowing in an inward turning, centripetal vortex receives and develops life energy, while outward turning, centrifugal, vortical motion disperses and destroys it. Using the counter-rotating vortex as a model, I could visualise the mechanism by which the energies of earth and sky focus to a point of intense concentration upon the summit of the Tor. The summit draws in matter

Non-Localised Seeing

The brain and the senses, such as sight and hearing, do not create consciousness and the ability to see and hear. Consciousness, seeing and hearing are *a priori*. They are properties of a pre-existing energy known as the self or the soul. The energy of the soul, through vortical movement, draws the biological forms to itself that create the body and the senses, but these mechanisms alone are not responsible for seeing, hearing or consciousness. As abilities of soul, these properties are not localised in an individual body, brain or human being. Consciousness and perception are the limited energy fields that can be received by the localised senses. The frequencies of light and sound perceived by the eye and ear create the impression of distinct and separate objects. Yet in meditation or heightened states it is possible to perceive in the manner described by mystics and now by quantum theory where there is no separation between subject and object.

The soul state of seeing for example is pure seeing. It is this state or the energy of seeing that creates sight. The biological mechanisms that form the eye and brain do not create sight. It is seeing that creates the eye, just as it is consciousness that creates the brain and not vice versa. In an out of body state – in a soul state – it is possible to experience seeing outside of the perceptual abilities of the sense organ of the eye. This is an altered state, however, and it can take time to adjust to seeing in this non-localised way. It is the physical senses that create the experience of individuality and separateness, while the soul senses create a unified, connected experience.

The scientist Rupert Sheldrake develops this theme in his concept of 'morphic fields'. These energy fields beyond our perception, he says, exist quite independently of brain mechanisms. The brain receives them rather than generates them, destroying the illusion of subject and object, the observer and the observed. This is supported by quantum physics where ideas like 'non-locality' reveal how energetic particles apparently separate in space retain a connectedness unpredicted by conventional science and can exist in many places at once.

through the path of energy from above and so shapes the hill below; conversely, the summit draws in energy through the shape of its hill and gives it form in the dimensions of the sky above. The matter of the summit is able to function in the manner of a beacon on the subtle energy levels as it was formed in a terrestrial mirror image of this process by the action of water and minerals over an immensely long period of geological time and is infused with water that is in a receptive state to creative life energy today.

The creative life energy of nature and the universe, the 'energy that cannot be created or destroyed', is not only described by engineers like Schauberger, by physicists like Sheldrake or Einstein, or by those who have studied the ancient wisdom like Dion Fortune, but it is also grasped through simple intuition. On the physical level, for example, I am instinctively attracted to the ratios of form that are natural, sustainable and generative. I describe these in the section on the vesica piscis and the Golden Section. On the emotional and mental level I am drawn to forms of logic, law, philosophy, architecture, art and ethics that come ever closer to balance, beauty, simplicity and truth. I intuitively know that the polarity and dualism in the manifest world are ultimately one. I know – without needing it to be explained to me because I can see it all around me – that the universe is a self-creating, self-sustaining intelligent system of energy, that through interdependent and interrelating polarity creates form in a manner that is always striving to achieve the most harmonious, perfect and beautiful expression of itself. This energy of life, the energy of the universe, flows through the channels and meridians it selects and shapes for itself in the perpetual dynamic of a beautifully structured, symmetrically patterned ingoing and outgoing dance. I also know, along with contemporary science, that the medium for this dance of life on earth is provided by water.

Although the above has always seemed like common sense to me, it was much harder for me to appreciate that it is the inner dance of energy that creates the outer forms that reveal it. I could not emphasise this point too strongly to myself in developing my understanding of the geophysical properties of water, the body and the Tor. I think developing my understanding of this was so difficult because I grew up in a mechanical world where I was taught external form came first and then, Frankenstein like, the energy is switched on to animate it. Matter, even sub-atomic particle matter, I was taught, is inert until energised. All machines are perceived like this, as are computers, and so is the medical view of the body (and so is the economy when reduced to value in the form of money, but that is another story). I had to drill the idea that energy is *a*

The Power of Water

In his book, *The Message from Water*, Masaru Emoto shows many photographs of water forming ice crystals as it freezes. He shows that the purer the water, the purer and more beautiful the ice crystals. City tap water for example rarely crystallises on freezing, but assumes dirty and random chaotic forms, while pure spring water easily develops colourful, exquisite and complex crystalline forms. Mr Emoto assumed this behaviour was due to the molecular structure of the water and that there was a direct correlation between a well developed crystalline structure and the purity of the water. He was surprised to discover that the crystallising ability of even severely polluted water was greatly enhanced by exposure to fine music, to prayer and even to kind words. The extraordinary conclusion was that water, when exposed to loving thoughts or sounds, rapidly reorganises its internal molecular structure into coherent and beautiful forms, and when exposed to negative thoughts and sounds quickly degenerates into amorphous shapes.

Mr Emoto thought that water everywhere is attempting to form the purest and most beautiful structure of itself possible. The underlying complex, hexagonal, molecular and crystalline structure of the basic element of life on earth is constantly striving to attain its most perfect expression. Through experiments with prayer and music Mr Emoto showed how even severely polluted water could attain this goal. Furthermore, he suggested that water in different locations with different properties, or on assuming these properties through collective intention, could accomplish different functions. It seemed to him for example, that the crystalline structure of the water from the fountain at Lourdes perfects itself into a form suitable for performing miracles because of the intentions of the millions of visitors who visit every year. Likewise water exposed to the name of the Japanese divine being Amarterasu assumes exquisite crystalline forms appropriate to the power of that deity.

priori into my head until I understood that energy itself flows and forms the shape it wants, rather than the shape is first created and then the energy is switched on to animate it. Indeed, I finally came to understand that the elementary particles of matter that form this world entirely consist of energy moving in continuous, stable vortices spinning at the speed of light. It is these vortices that create Sheldrake's 'morphic fields' as it is their energy that is responsible for time and space.[3]

Observation of water provides many examples of energy shaping the form it wants to flow in. Over the aeons water has moulded the forms of earth into shapes most conducive for its passage. Water is most unhappy when made to flow in straight lines. When water flows in straight lines it loses its vibrant life-enhancing qualities, while water allowed to naturally flow in self-formed, sinuous, in–turning, vortical and cycloid channels vibrates with life-enhancing energy. The work of Japanese researcher Masaru Emoto shows it is the energy within water that is responsible for the form it demonstrates in the world. Under strict laboratory conditions, Emoto photographed water at the moment of freezing. When the water was pure its ice crystals were correspondingly pure. When the water was impure, it crystallised into lifeless and ugly forms.[4]

From my experience and my research I came to understand that there are many examples of this process in the natural world. The energy of life moving into a form such as a tree attempts to shape the growing tree in a pattern that is most expressive of its internal, life-harmonising qualities. The tree literally vibrates in sympathy with its surroundings. It is sensitive to light, heat, cold, touch, shadow, gravity, moisture and so on, as its internal energy unfolds in relation to its surroundings to give it form. The proportions of the Golden Section prescribe the ratios of this form. The human body also contains forms such as channels and nerves that are made by and reveal the nature of the energy passing through them. The colon is shaped by the nature of the energy, in this case the food, passing through it. The arteries, veins and the ventricles of the heart are shaped by the nature of the blood; the nerves and brain are shaped by electrical impulses, while the nasal passages and lungs are shaped by the nature of air. All these energies are in a constant dance of diastole and systole, inbreath and outbreath, intake and elimination, and through this dance they efficiently shape and maintain the biological organism in harmony with the whole.

I also understand that after Einstein it became impossible for science to view the world as matter simply responding to mechanical laws. Einstein showed that matter was equivalent to energy, $E = m$, while the amount of energy in matter is expressed by the speed of light squared, c^2. Indeed, scientists who study quantum physics today say that atoms themselves are not solid, but can be described entirely in terms of their complex energetic charges. The universe, the world, life and the human body, are formed from the vibrant interaction of energetic forces. The great contribution of quantum physics to scientific thinking is its ability to describe the previously invisible connection between apparently separate things, to examine the interdependence of mind and matter, earth and soul, the observer and the observed.

The important breakthrough came on the day when I realised that the human body is itself an energy channel, a 'mortal coil', for the passage of the soul through life. The soul is energy on a journey of incoming and outgoing. The body – which is mostly water – takes its shape around the incoming energy of the soul and loses its shape as the soul returns to its eternal home. The matter that forms the brain is the receiver of the energy of consciousness, not the generator of it, and if the brain can grow in conditions most conducive to its full development, so consciousness can fully take up its home. Water is the medium *par excellence* of receptivity and when the energised atmosphere around the incoming and outgoing soul is conducive for transition then the energy of the soul can fulfil itself most effectively. The soul in transition is aided by the harmonious intentions and the quality of vibrational forces around it. These form a 'seed bed' – an energetic pattern most sensitised to and apparent in the vibrating forms of water – from which the soul can draw the constituent components for the manifestation of complete and exquisite forms. The soul energy is supported through a sympathetic vortical medium to achieve a structure most expressive of its true and infinite nature in the same way as water is supported to create optimum conditions of purity, complexity and interaction for the development of life on earth through its flow in vortex forms. As the energy in the molecules of Mr. Emoto's water was enhanced by prayerful intent to form full expressions of itself – as evidenced by its complex crystallising forms – so the energy of the soul can be supported by loving and intelligent intent to assume its most complete and dynamic form by a vortex especially created and maintained for the purpose.

It is the research of those like Emoto and Sheldrake that makes the positive link between the receptive and energetic qualities of water and the intelligent energy of the mind. It demonstrates the mechanism whereby the water held in the aquifer of the soul portal of Avalon can assume an energy vortex appropriate for the process of soul transition and transformation when enhanced by positive intention. Those people in the past who understood the ability of the vibrating molecules and the ionic energy fields of the water in the Tor to respond to prayers, toning and visualisations gathered here to conduct practices that specifically supported this function.

According to the psychometrist Iris Campbell, 'the contemplative order or monks drawn to this ancient site of Glaston – knowing as they did of these terrestrial-cum-celestial mysteries – made it their life's work to pray for the peace of the world. This they did by projecting their thoughts into the seething underworld'.[5] A literal reading of the myths around the Red Spring suggests one of the methods employed by the monks to carry out this practice. The myths say that the waters of the spring turned red with 'the healing blood of Christ' when the cup used at the Last Supper was buried in the ground nearby. The cup used at the Last Supper was the vessel in which the liquid within it was transformed into the blood of Christ. The cup is the vessel in which other substances – especially receptive liquids such as water – are transformed into other states, and moreover, highly beneficial states. Research into blood reveals that it is the iron in the blood, in the form of haemoglobin that, when potentised by oxygen via the mediating effect of the essential amino acids, carries energy to every part of the body. This suggests that it is the iron in the water of the Red or Blood Spring that, when potentised by the restructuring of the ionic charges of its atoms through sympathetic intention or blessing, carries energy into the heart of the transformational system held in the aquifer beneath the Tor. The Tor, in this Christian mythos, is the cup or the chalice of transformation. The vortical energy that forms the element of iron anchors the transformational process of coming into and going out of being in the atomic dance of the cosmos. The vortical element that is hydrogen orchestrates the dance, oxygen feeds it and all the other elements play their part. In the here and now of the soul's cosmic presence and awareness, it is the vortical molecular pattern and core provided by the element of iron – that the ancients named blood and the Christian monks held at the heart of the mystery of transubstantiation – that carries the life force in, through and out of being on earth.

ENTRANCEWAY

The dynamic of the Tor assumes the form of a central axis around which turns a complex vortex of energy. The water bearing aquifer, given external shape by the hill and the terraces on its flanks, manifests the internal energy of this vortex. As it is possible to conceive of this pattern being mirrored in the sky, or rather in a pure unmanifested energetic form, there are therefore two vortices, with whatever internal dynamics they contain, meeting at a point on the summit of the Tor. This is the point of equilibrium and of convergence where it becomes possible for one energy to transform into another and for new, vortical, light, time and space dynamics to begin. A ramp now can be added to this picture, formed by the horizontal axis of the Tor, extending south-westwards. When viewed from above, the cone of the Tor is given an elongated shape by this ramp, and when viewed from the ground, the incline of the ramp provides the obvious means of access. It provides an entranceway. This entranceway adds an important component to the dynamic of the Tor.

The internal reciprocating energies of the Tor are made accessible by an entrance, which begins at the pair of springs at its foot. This entrance approach is like the ramp beside a ziggurat, a pyramid, or some other comparable image of the world mountain. The line of entrance extends over the surrounding plain and is marked by another conical hill, Burrowbridge Mump eleven miles away, and by orientation to the rising and setting sun on the cross-quarter days. The horizontal axis or extension of the Tor is also crucial for the labyrinthine pattern upon the slopes – any other shape would not allow the classical labyrinth design to work. The explicit entrance imagery deepens the designation of the Tor in the Avalonian tradition as the portal between the worlds.

As a positively charged, centripetal, in-turning vortex increases in energy as it comes to the centre of its system, the centre (or the edge of centre) contains more latent energy than any other point in the system. The energy of a natural vortex increases here and then has to be released in some manner. In theory the amount of energy concentrated in a centri-petal vortical system is infinite, while the mass is zero. The obvious manner for the release of energy concentrated in a system of this sort is in radiant bursts of energy in the form of light, moving outward from the centre. The description of the dynamic of the Tor in the writings of psychics and visionaries is that of energy radiating outward from the summit in visible bursts of light along its horizontal axes. Another psychometrist Olive Pixley, a contemporary of Iris Campbell, described the raising of a vortex of energy by people walking the terraces. This met with a vortex descending from the sun, and the resultant energy shot out through 'the alignments' over the land.[6] Ley line researchers report many such horizontal alignments passing through Glastonbury Tor. Some of these alignments are local, others are global, some have astronomical significance and some do not.

The total image of the dynamic of the Tor now becomes clear: Subtle energies descending and ascending in centripetal, spiral and

complex manifold vortexes focused along a vertical axis onto the summit of the Tor where they generate centrifugal forces of different qualities. These forces extend outward, and flow along horizontal axes in radiant bursts, while one axis provides the chief means of access to and from the central place of converging power.

ALIGNMENTS

The evidence of construction undertaken in prehistory to emphasise and enhance the sun, moon and star alignments to and from the Tor show that astronomical alignments were considered to add to the energetic qualities of Avalon. The island, surrounded by a plain with

▲ Tor energy

Exercise: The Energy of the Axis Mundi

To experience the energy of the world axis I recommend the following exercise. It is as though the practitioner becomes a mini-Tor!

Stand in a place where the energies of earth and sky are clear and strong. It can be indoors or out. Relax the body. It is helpful to prepare the body through stretching or other physical activity.

Visualise the energies of the earth as a vortex whose circumference extends into the surroundings. It can be near or far away. The important thing is to see the vortex having a centripetal or inward turning motion. It does not matter which way the vortex turns as long as it turns inwards to the centre. Note: a spinning object will appear to turn in one direction when viewed from above and in the other when viewed from below, so direction is unimportant unless for specific reasons clockwise or counter-clockwise is selected.

At the same time, visualise the energies of the sky moving in a vortex whose circumference starts near or far away. Again, it is an inward turning centripetal vortex, but this vortex is in contra-rotation to the one below. When the distant motion of these two vortices is established, visualise them both coming to the centre. The energy of the earth vortex may rise as it approaches the body and the energy of the sky vortex may descend.

As the two vortices of contra-rotating energy approach the body, allow them to increase. The energy of each vortex intensifies and moves faster and faster. As they reach maximum spin and intensity, visualise the vortices as two concentrated spheres of energy approaching and meeting in the centre of the body. Allow them to meet.

Allow the energy of their meeting to disperse throughout the psychophysical system. The practitioner may feel that this exercise releases energy for healing or for another purpose. Like a vortex of water, this is an intensely receptive practice that carries the energy of the earth and sky of that particular time and place. It can therefore be practised anywhere. As the practitioner becomes more skilful, it is possible to add to the contra-rotating energy vortices other energy dynamics. Manifold energies can be introduced, in the same manner as different molecules are formed by the combination of vortices of different elements, or, on a greater scale, different solar systems are formed by the vortices of a variety of planets. The introduction of sound can enhance the process. Practitioners may notice the affinity between this exercise and magical traditions such as casting a circle or raising a cone of power.

its distant horizon, formed a perfect centre for viewing the sky, while the Tor and the hills of the island were complemented by the addition of an earthen mound sited for the best observation of celestial events. Although the rule was not to build upon the isle, the construction of the mound – like the first work upon the Tor – was either so far back in time that it was carried out before the rule became established or because it was considered essential to work with the energy of the island in combination with the heavenly cycles.

The list of alignments that follows is not exhaustive. They are alignments to astronomical events the people of the past most often observed and marked. If the reader wishes to pursue the main thread of the book, this section can be returned to later.[7]

1. The East-West Alignment of Dod Lane (90° and 180°). This line is oriented to the rising and the setting sun at the equinoxes. On the Isle of Avalon it is marked by a pre-Christian road of the dead upon which the Mary Chapel, the Abbey Church and St. Benedict's Church (circled) were subsequently located. *Dod*=aged, dead. This alignment continued eastwards points toward other ancient sites including Stonehenge; continued westwards it points toward the sea. An east–west equinox line of this nature marks the balance of night and day, of the seasons, of time and space – the equal and ordered division of the world.

2. The Abbey, Chalice Hill, Tor Alignment (100°). From the earliest foundation in the Abbey grounds – the 'Old Church' or the Mary Chapel (circled) – there is a precise alignment to the Tor over the summit of Chalice Hill. The sun can be observed rising on this alignment on 27 September, the feast day of St. Michael or Michaelmas, and on 17 March, the feast day of St. Patrick and Joseph of Arimathea – the main patron saints of Glastonbury.

3. The St. Michael Line or Cross Quarter Day Alignment (63° and 243°). The axis of the Tor is aligned to the rising sun on the cross quarter days of Beltane, 1 May, and Lughnasadh, 1 August, and to the setting sun on the corresponding cross quarter days of Samhain, 31 October, and Imbolc, 1 February. The cross quarter days lie midway between the solstices and the equinoxes and were the significant festival days of the Celtic year. This alignment continues eleven miles southwest to Burrowbridge Mump, a conical hill similar to the Tor with a church upon its summit, before passing on to other sites including St. Michael's

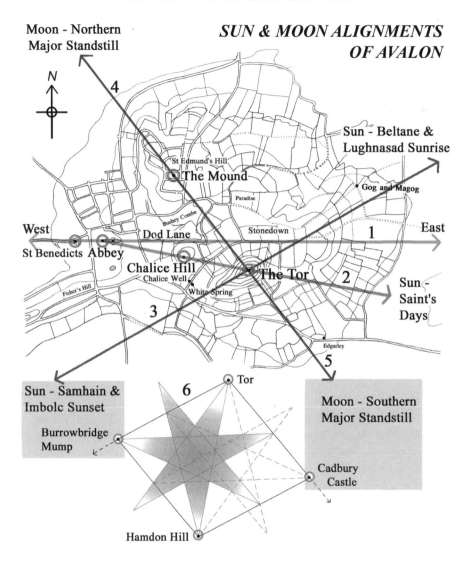

SUN & MOON ALIGNMENTS OF AVALON

Moon - Northern Major Standstill

Sun - Beltane & Lughnasad Sunrise

West

East

Sun - Saint's Days

Sun - Samhain & Imbolc Sunset

Moon - Southern Major Standstill

St Benedicts Abbey

St Edmund's Hill

The Mound

Paradise

Bushey Combe

Dod Lane

Stonedown

Gog and Magog

Chalice Hill

Chalice Well

Fisher's Hill

White Spring

The Tor

Edgarley

Burrowbridge Mump

Tor

Cadbury Castle

Hamdon Hill

Mount in Cornwall. The alignment continued northeast points to other ancient sites including Avebury.

4. **The Major Standstill Alignment** (320° and 140°). Intersecting the St. Michael Line at the Tor is an alignment to the most northerly setting and the most southerly rising point of the moon. From the Mound (circled), an artificial earthwork on St. Edmund's Hill to the northwest of the Tor, the observer can see the full moon rise on the shoulder south of the summit of the Tor at its most southerly rising

point. The moon takes 18.61 years to move through a complete cycle of extreme rising and setting points known as the major standstills. The Mound is precisely placed to observe this phenomenon, both from it to the Tor for the most southerly moonrise and from it to the Mendip Hills and to distant mountains in Wales (when visible) for the most northerly moonset. The next major standstill is in 2006.[8] For the observers upon an isle of the dead, these extreme positions taken by the moon in the sky were of utmost significance. The long cyclical journey to and from the points of greatest and least moonlight in the night sky promised eternal return, recurrence and rebirth.

5. Arthur's Hunting Path (320° and 140°). The lunar alignment described above when extended southeast continues 11 miles to South Cadbury hill fort – commonly known as Cadbury Castle, the most likely contender for King Arthur's Camelot. Legend says he and the Wild Hunt ride 'Arthur's Hunting Path' to the Tor every few years. As this path is aligned to the extreme rising and setting points of the moon it is probable the hunt rides along it every 18.61 years. In essence, the observer can see from Cadbury the most northerly setting point of the moon over the Tor, and from the Tor the most southerly rising point of the moon over Cadbury. As described in the section on Celtic Avalon where a burial at Cadbury is oriented to the Tor, this alignment indicates another road of the dead. The Cadbury, Tor, Mound, Mendip, Welsh mountain line is an outstanding astronomical alignment, as it combines the dominant geographical features of the area with human developed ones to emphasise the most extreme rising and setting points of the 18.61 year lunar cycle.

6. The Tor-Mump-Cadbury-Hamdon Hill Diamond. The cross quarter day and the major standstill alignments at this latitude (51° N) intersect at an angle of 77.14° or 102.86°. This creates a ratio of 3 to 4. When developed into a rhombus (an equal sided parallelogram) from the placement of the eleven miles equidistant sites of Burrowbridge Mump, Cadbury Castle and Hamdon Hill – sites of great prehistorical and historical significance for the area – the basis is formed for that most difficult to generate of figures, the heptagram or the seven-pointed star. All these sites are visible from Glastonbury Tor, if not from each other, and the keen awareness of landscape held by the people of the past makes it likely that this remarkable relationship was noticed. Indeed, the legend of Arthur's Hunting Path and the deliberate placement of the Mound provide firm evidence for the knowledge of astronomy and geometry involved.[9]

A second set of sun and moon alignments are observable from the earth mound built upon the summit of St. Edmund's or Windmill Hill. There is controversy around this site, simply known as the Mound, as some say it is natural or was built recently and others say it is a 17th century windmill mound. Maps however show the Mound existed before 1900 CE, and the evidence of the alignments advances the case for the Mound being much more than a base for a windmill. It was a site for viewing and marking astronomical events in prehistory. The events observed from the Mound are similar to those of Stonehenge, with which it shares an identical latitude, except that they employ natural rather than artificial features. As archaeology has found little upon the Isle of Avalon that can be firmly attributed to prehistory, if the hypothesis presented here for the Mound is correct then it has enormous implications for the early use and meaning of the Isle of Avalon.

7 & 9. The Winter Solstice Alignments (129° and 231°). The Mound on St. Edmund's Hill is located to observe the extreme positions of the moon and the extreme positions of the rising and setting sun at the solstices. When the area was clear of trees, which appears to be the case in prehistory, an observer upon the Mound saw the sun rise on and around the Winter Solstice, 21 December, at the base of the Tor and then move up its northern flank. This is a dramatic spectacle and one that frequently attracted the attention of prehistoric astronomers and megalithic/mound builders.

It appears the 30 metre wide by 40 plus metre long (oriented on a north–south axis) Mound was placed and elevated above the surrounding broad hilltop precisely for the purpose of making this and other observations. The surveyor, Alexander Thom – who commented in the 1960s on the usefulness of the features in the Tor/Stonedown area for celestial observation – said that the area merited the title of a 'megalithic observatory', but he never provided the evidence for this. Thom described stones in the correct location on Stonedown for viewing the sunrise at the base of the Tor from the Mound, but these stones have disappeared and the current landowner has no recollection of them. The stones are marked on the Ordnance Survey Map of 1902, but the only one that remains is a typical 19th century field boundary marker.[10] Apparently Thom did not fully include the Mound in his calculations, perhaps because it is ringed with trees, or more likely, because he believed the common explanation that the Mound was built in the 17th century as a base for a windmill. Thom did however note that the most northerly setting point of the moon was at an azimuth of precisely 320° in 1700 BC

SUN AND MOON ALIGNMENTS FROM THE MOUND - ST EDMUNDS HILL, GLASTONBURY

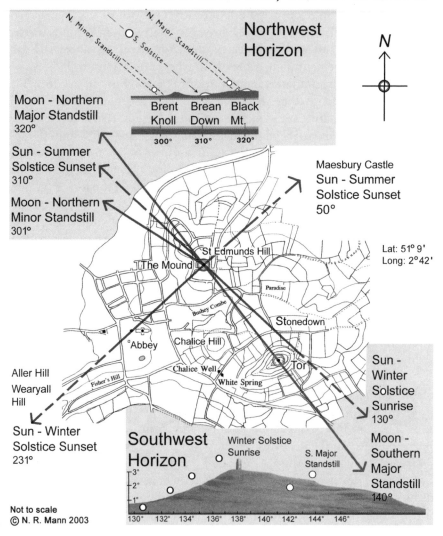

Northwest Horizon

N

Moon - Northern Major Standstill 320°

Brent Knoll 300°
Brean Down 310°
Black Mt. 320°

Sun - Summer Solstice Sunset 310°

Moon - Northern Minor Standstill 301°

N. Minor Standstill
O S. Solstice
N. Major Standstill

Maesbury Castle
Sun - Summer Solstice Sunset 50°

St Edmunds Hill
The Mound

Paradise

Lat: 51° 9'
Long: 2° 42'

Bushey Combe

Stonedown

Abbey
Chalice Hill

Aller Hill
Wearyall Hill

Fisher's Hill

Chalice Well
White Spring

Tor

Sun - Winter Solstice Sunrise 130°

Sun - Winter Solstice Sunset 231°

Southwest Horizon

Winter Solstice Sunrise

S. Major Standstill

-3°
-2°
-1°

Moon - Southern Major Standstill 140°

Not to scale
© N. R. Mann 2003

130° 132° 134° 136° 138° 140° 142° 144° 146°

from this latitude, and the alignment from the Tor to the Black Mountain in Wales, which he suggests marks this important event, passes directly over the Mound.[11]

Not only does the Winter Solstice sun rise in this dramatic manner when viewed from the Mound but it also sets on another remarkable alignment. At Winter Solstice the sun sets directly over the flank of

Aller Hill by High Ham, itself visible directly over the western end of Wearyall Hill. This forms a striking alignment of natural features but one that is now unfortunately entirely obscured by buildings. What makes the Winter Solstice alignments from the Mound especially impressive is their relationship to the three other sacred hills of Avalon. The round belly of Chalice Hill lies to the south of the Mound, mirroring on the earth the zenith of the progression of the sun as its arcs through the sky. This correspondence is especially noticeable at Winter Solstice when the sun takes its lowest path through the sky. In essence, the winter sun rises over the head of the Tor, passes over the belly of Chalice Hill and sets beneath the feet of Wearyall Hill – outlining features with more than a passing resemblance to a body. Further observation may also show that the features on the flanks of the Tor were cut to mark the most southerly rising positions of the sun and moon.

9 & 10. **The Summer Solstice Alignments** (50° and 310°). Directly opposite the Winter Solstice alignments on the horizon are the extreme rising and setting points of the sun at the Summer Solstice. If, for example, an observer stood in the location Thom gave for the now missing stones on Stonedown, the Summer Solstice sunset is visible (or was before trees grew to obscure it) over the Mound at Brean Down on the northwest horizon. The Mound is precisely placed to observe the northernmost setting points of sun and moon on the most prominent features of the western horizon. The group of hills Brent Knoll, Steep Holm, Brean Down, Bleadon Hill and Crook Peak form a pronounced range of features for precise observation of these events. Of course, the observer can also see these events from the summit of the Tor, but, with the exception of the Black Mountain in Wales, without the degree of accuracy that wooden or stone back-sights located around the Mound made possible.

The second Summer Solstice alignment is toward the rising sun. For an observer upon the Mound, the sun on and around 21 June rises over Maesbury Castle on the southeastern horizon. Maesbury is an important Iron Age hillfort on the Mendip Hills. Directly below Maesbury and closer to Avalon is the prominent Launcherly or Dragon Hill. Dragon Legends are associated with this hill, giving the name to the nearby village of Worminster (*worm*=dragon).

What is especially significant about this alignment is that in the same manner as the inhabitants of Cadbury Castle could see an extreme astronomical event take place over the Tor (the northern major standstill), so the inhabitants of Maesbury could observe the sun set into the Isle of

Avalon at the Winter Solstice. The winter sun passes low over the very steeply profiled Tor and sets into the island over the Mound. The Mound was constructed on a scale for it to be visible from Maesbury. The western flank of Aller Hill is also visible beyond the Mound. This alignment establishes a connection between Avalon and the prehistoric people of the area. It is evident from a visit to Maesbury that the hill top site is placed with an eye to Avalon. It is a pleasant congruence that Aller Hill, like Launcherly Hill, has strong dragon traditions associated with it. Local legend says that a dragon regularly flew between Aller and Curry Rivel, a path that lies directly upon this solstice alignment. Could this legend retain a memory from the Iron Age or from even earlier?[12]

Maesbury, Launcherly Hill, the Mound, Wearyall Hill and Aller Hill combine to provide an outstanding astronomical alignment in the area that incorporates natural with intentionally placed prehistoric features. The fact that the Mary Chapel of Glastonbury Abbey also lies exactly on this alignment, and that at least two places along its length possess dragon legends, show that awareness of this solstice line was likely to have carried on into history.

11. The Minor Standstill Alignments (301° and 120°). The location of the Mound also allows observation of the moon at the midpoints in its 18.61 year cycle to and from its extreme northern and southern rising and setting points. These midpoints are known as the Minor Standstills. Brent Knoll on the northwestern horizon from the Mound for example provides an excellent marker for observation of the northern minor standstill of the setting moon. Observers on the Mound could use Brent Knoll and just beyond it, the isle of Steep Holm in the Bristol Channel, to track the moon as it progressed further and further away from the axis or the ecliptic of the sun. This was important, as the times when the moon crossed the ecliptic of the sun were the times when an eclipse was most likely to occur. Conversely, observers on the Iron Age hill fort on Brent Knoll could use the distant Isle of Avalon with its several hills to track the rising moon on its passage between the standstills. They also saw the Winter Solstice sunrise in the notch between Chalice Hill and Wearyall Hill. It is events like these, all dealing with the extreme positions of the sun and moon, viewed from the hill forts and centres of significance in prehistory, that build up a picture of how the people of the time thought and felt about the Isle of Avalon.

The 51° north latitude of the Isle of Avalon means that the alignments of the major standstills and the solstices intersect at an angle of 90°. Knowledge of this right angle is brought out at Stonehenge where

The Mound - Windmill Hill

Dundon Beacon

▲ A favourable comparison can be made between the Mound on Windmill Hill and the early Bronze Age barrow on Dundon Hill. Although the Mound is slightly larger, the hill top position, the similar profile and close proximity make it likely they were built about the same time.

the major axes of the monument are oriented to these events through the deliberate use of a rectangle. Whether this was of interest to the astronomers of the Isle of Avalon is unclear, but the 3 to 4 ratio of the intersection of the cross-quarter day and major standstill alignments is brought out in the arrangement of Cadbury, Hamdon Hill, Burrow-bridge and the Tor.

Although no excavations or geophysical surveys have been carried out on the Mound, the astronomical information provided here makes the case for the Mound being an extremely important example of intentional construction upon the Isle of Avalon in prehistory. The late Neolithic period or the early Bronze Age is the most likely period for the construction of the Mound, 3000–1700 BCE – contemporary with the similar alignments at Stonehenge – but only excavation could confirm this. If postholes were found in the original ground level of the Mound, or fore-sights and back-sights found nearby that revealed orientation to astronomical events and features on the horizon, then the case would be confirmed. There is a similar Bronze Age barrow on Dundon Beacon, about four miles south of Glastonbury. The barrow is considered to be an outlier from the Mendip group and occupies a position on a prominent hilltop that became an Iron Age hill fort. The fact that it is there supports the case for the Mound being a prehistoric barrow, and although the Dundon barrow lacks the astronomical sophistication of the Mound, the Mound and the Tor are highly visible from it. It appears that the Bronze and Iron Age features of the area align themselves to Avalon in a significant manner; but establishing exactly what this significance was is not easy.

The marking of the solar solstice and the lunar standstill alignments on the Isle of Avalon reveal the keen interest taken by the builders of the Mound in events at the extremes of cycles – events fundamental to transformation on a cosmic scale. The Winter Solstice for example, when combined with a southern lunar standstill event, creates an intense contrast with a time of light. Observation of the turning points at these times is critical. Observation made it possible to understand the patterns of the cosmos and align terrestrial events to them. The extreme points obtained by the celestial bodies mark time and space, night and day, summer and winter, the rhythmic paths of energy and of light. Their turning around the *axis mundi* of Avalon forms the point of connection in the dynamic relationship between the human and the Other, the heavenly worlds.

THE JOURNEY INTO THE AVALONIAN DREAMTIME

One of the tasks of the school on the Isle of Avalon was to initiate candidates into the spiritual mysteries of the soul and its journey to the Otherworld. In prehistory, before the Druids emerged to offer a broad and organised basis for this specialised teaching, those who had undertaken it through their local shamanic lineage recommended the initiation. From about 400 BCE, as the Druid Orders emerged in the pan-European age of the Celts, Avalon came under their jurisdiction and they selected candidates for initiation upon the island. Perhaps this was part of the training for a Druidic Order, or perhaps the afterlife mysteries were open to everyone. Later, in history, there is the strong possibility that Avalon as an initiatory mystery school was recognised and continued by the Romans, the post-Roman British and even by the Anglo-Saxons for a period before the widespread conversion to Christianity. The school could perform its work as long as it lent no power to the Druids and paid its taxes like everyone else. It received patronage from wealthy local landowners in the same manner as they supported the nearby temples at Lamyatt, Brean Down, Cadbury Castle and Cadbury Congresbury. There is the suggestion of a circular temple on the Tor, but the evidence also shows that a temple was unlikely to have stood for long before being removed.[13] There is also the possibility that the school came under duress in the early Christian period, and so its teachings became occult.

The main purpose of the school on the Isle of Avalon was to teach the mysteries of the soul: its immortal or universal nature, its incarnation in life, its transformation in death, and the journey into the afterlife and rebirth. It did this in two ways: through practices concerned with guiding souls through the portal to the Otherworld and through initiatory journeys that taught these mysteries. The first practices were concerned with the passage of recently deceased souls into the afterlife, the second with teaching the mysteries in this life. The following sections describe these practices, beginning with the teaching journey.

INITIATORY JOURNEY

The first opportunity for an initiatory journey was at the time of coming of age. It was undertaken when the candidates were sexually ready. Although the preparation and assimilation processes differed according to gender, the soul mysteries at the heart of the Avalonian initiation were essentially the same. The candidates were taken across the inland sea in a barge – a flat-bottomed boat. These boats could easily slide through the large expanses of shallow and reed-filled water. Examples of these boats come from the Lake Villages at Glastonbury and Meare.[14] The inland sea of the Summerland was alive with otters, frogs, fish and fowl. Swans glided through the still waters. The air was thick with birds, especially in the migration seasons, and the reed beds vibrated with their song as they settled for the night.

If possible, the candidates were taken across the waters at a time and under circumstances conducive to their sexual arousal. The barge was draped with beautiful materials that they were unlikely to see in their everyday lives. Those guiding the boat were cloaked, adorned, and understood the nature and the power of glamour. Indeed, the understanding of glamour was a vital component of the curriculum of a school so close to the infinitely seductive beauty of the fairy world. Its members knew it was the music barely heard, the taste scarcely suggested, the loveliness only just seen, that evoked the deepest longings and memories of the soul.

According to the age and needs of the candidates they were given food and drink upon the journey. In most cases the candidates were required to fast and the drink contained herbs to help and sustain them. When appropriate, the drink contained a mild psychotropic substance such as psylocibin derived from the indigenous 'Liberty Cap' mushroom; but usually this was unnecessary, as the candidates were stimulated enough by the occasion and the natural surroundings for the inner processes to unfold.

The marshes themselves held wonders. First, there were the lights. In Somerset folklore the lights – perhaps from marsh gases – hovering over the surface of the marshes, were not lost souls, but the light of their guides. The 'Punkie' lights, the original Halloween lanterns, guided the souls of the recently deceased to Avalon. Then there were the mists. The 'White Lady' came in mysterious ways – long, searching tendrils creeping over the waters, thick impenetrable vapours that stopped at tree level, broiling masses rolling over hillsides – and then departed as strangely as she came.

As the barge neared the island echoes of faint music were heard. Lovely sights were seen shimmering on the shore. Again, these only needed suggestion, as the stimulated senses and imagination of the candidate provided the rest. Twilight at sunset or dawn provided the perfect opportunity for this kind of glamour to be cast. The island, untouched by axe and plough, or by the weapons of the hunter, and with its extraordinary hills rising above the wooded slopes, lent itself to the scene. It is likely that the swans and other waterfowl along the shore were tame, and the sacred and wild animals of the place were familiar with the comings and goings of the school. The candidates were silently invited to disembark on reaching the shore. The initiation was undertaken in verbal silence. The school knew its teachings went beyond the language of specific time and place, and if needed, a single word of guidance was usually sufficient.

It is now up to the members of the school to play their role. Two women – priestesses or initiatrixes – guide the candidate along the path into the centre of the island. They are beautifully dressed, and have cast a glamour around themselves that allows them to act as a powerful catalyst to the experience of the candidate. It does not matter how the priestesses really look. To the candidate, on the occasion of coming of age, they are sexually exciting, erotic, mysterious and otherworldly.

They proceed through the woods on the lower slopes of the island. There are animals among the trees. Perhaps creatures from the sacred herd show themselves – the red or white cattle of the native British breeds. From time to time the silhouette of the hills in the centre of the island appear against the sky. If the candidate has psychic abilities then beings from other realms might appear. They move higher and directly toward the verdant valley between the two most dramatic hills. The path is more or less straight. It may wind from side to side, but there is an increasing sense of urgency and progress toward the destination emerging directly ahead. They arrive at the base of the valley. There are two streams flowing on either side. There is the rubeate water of the Red Spring bubbling up under artesian pressure from within the earth and there is the source of the White Spring in its dark cave reaching under the Tor.

When ready, the candidate stops. The body is unable to go any further without, so the forward moving energy, now physically checked, takes awareness within. The candidate moves deeper into universal awareness as it passes into the recesses of the vale beneath the Tor. It passes through a threshold that appears according to the subjective conditioning of a lifetime's experience. The threshold might appear as a cave, as a tunnel or a temple door. It might be lights, sounds, or a whole multitude of sensations evoked by the Avalonian journey. The priestesses on either side stimulate and keep the initiate on course. They know the journey is as much into the inner landscape of the eternal soul as it is into the heart of Avalon. Their task is to synchronise the inner and the outer, so the life of the individual soul is attuned to the soul of all life. They ensure for example, that the unfolding or emerging energy within the candidate is directed through the central channel of the psychosomatic or neurological system rather than through the channels to the left or the right hand side. This is made explicit by the entranceway to the Tor, the ridge that defines the ascent and entry on the southwest path, running directly from here to the centre of the energy held by the summit, and by the openings in the lines of trees and terraces that cross it. The techniques used synchronised the vortex patterns of energy focused by the Tor with the energies held in the fluid of the spinal column.

Initiates who are practised, or have undergone the journey several times, are far more comfortable with the complex network of forces about them. The enormously powerful Devic and elemental forces that shape life on earth for example are consciously accessible only to some. For others, the sexually creative forces held in the emergent energy of the cellular DNA are overwhelming and carry them swiftly through the inner world with little attention to detail. There is a rush toward rebirth. For yet others, the experience is dominated by the psychic, mental and emotional dualism of the corporeal nature. If there is unclarity around this dualism in life, perhaps due to stifling social consensus or religious belief, or over-reliance on one portion of the brain, simply having to face and resolve these energies with the whole being immediately upon death can produce a traumatic experience. Hence the need to practise the journey beforehand.

The details of the inner journey are determined by the unique contents of each individual mind as they are constellated upon the collective archetypal background. Due to varied cultural conditioning and the karmic and life experience of the soul it is impossible to describe any one subjective experience, but it is possible to describe the transpersonal archetypal content of the journey from the descriptions of those who have undertaken it and returned to tell the tale. People usually report that the journey into the Otherworld, either undertaken through an initiatory process or through an out of body or near-death experience (NDE), usually provides them with an intense sense of well being, of peace, of light and of supportive guidance. Relatives or friends appear as guiding spirit figures. There are descriptions of immensely wise and powerful beings who provide assistance and love. There is sometimes a review of the past and sometimes a scene of judgement; but above all, those who have undergone a NDE report a deep and profound sense of understanding and of being understood, of there being a purpose and a meaning to it all. There is a sense of dissolving into a greater universe, into a place where the self or consciousness is released from a lesser, restricted state into a boundless, infinite one. Scientific research into the NDE is still in its early days, but so far investigators say the evidence supports experience after clinical death. The view they are developing of the brain, they say, is not one of a producer but of a receiver of consciousness. The experience of meaning, of understanding, of truth and so on, is not a function produced by a mechanical collection of cells but arises from elsewhere.[15]

For those whose task it was to take people into the Otherworld through the Avalonian portal, this knowledge would come as no surprise. Their goal was to show how the individual life experience of the soul that comes through the physical senses dissolves into the far greater awareness of the soul of all life at death – individual consciousness dissolves into cosmic consciousness, might be one way of putting it. Whatever the description, the candidates return to this life experience under the guidance of the initiated priestesses. It might be a slow process. The mind may be scattered and may wander off somewhere into the fairy, animal or elemental realms. The priestesses were skilled however, any deluding glamours were put aside, and the candidates were grounded back into the body with food, drink and everyday conversation. Having undergone the journey once the candidates were unlikely to forget it, and the sense of understanding, meaning and purpose acquired served them in good stead when the time came to make the journey at the time of death.

THE BEACON FOR THE DEAD

The second practice of the school on the Isle of Avalon was to maintain and enhance the function of the guiding beacon upon the Tor for those crossing over into the next life. The Tor – along with other places around the world – appears to discarnate souls as a specific location upon the earth where they can cross over to the Otherworld. The Tor has an energetic, emergent and generative presence in the collective consciousness or the collective soul of life.

In this book I try to explain the geophysical mechanism that accounts for this quality – the existence of the *axis mundi*, the aquifer in the Tor, the dynamic properties of the hydrogen atom, of water, of vortices and so on – but, failing an adequate rational explanation, it just might be that the portal is here because the intelligence of the universe chooses to maintain it here and not because of any natural reason. The portal is here because it was thought this is the place for just such a portal and people have continued to hold this view ever since. The school certainly did not worry itself over explanations. It knew it had work to do that was easier done here than elsewhere. It got on with the task of enhancing the soul beacon, the pathways to and from it, and providing guidance for those using it.

I was told by the water dowser I asked to investigate the aquifer, that the 'Punkies', the lights guiding the souls of the deceased to the portal upon the Isle of Avalon, were created through the piezo-electrical qualities of the 'crystal resonance chamber' within the Tor. The electrical qualities of the aquifer were directed through the resonance chamber and then out along the alignments over the land. Although this was easier to accomplish at times when the aquifer was strongly charged by atmospheric and telluric currents, the main key, she said, to sending the energy – visible as light – along the alignments, was through 'the power of mental concentration enhanced by vibrational toning'. It was necessary she said, 'to visualise the core of energy within the Tor building a charge through the chamber, and to visualise the alignments readying themselves to receive this charge'. The core, its swirling sheaves of energy and the lines extending outwards over the land, were then activated by toning directed from a distance into the chamber. This built up a vibratory resonance within the chamber that increased the charge until it no longer could be held and was released outward. The greater the ability to hold the focus and build the energy through toning, the greater the ability for the energy to travel for great distances along the alignments or 'spirit paths' described in the previous section. The energy appeared on these paths as lights guiding the soul to the portal on Avalon.

The location of the places for visualisation and toning were not upon the Tor itself, she thought, but at the entrances to the tunnels under the Tor. Although it is clear that the cave at the White Spring provided just such an access point, the evidence shows that toning was also done in what is now the Abbey grounds. The legends of tunnels running from there to the Tor, and of chanting monks entering them or projecting thoughts into them, are too many to dismiss. Glastonbury can claim to be a location for a 'perpetual choir', that is, monks chanting in shifts twenty-four hours a day. It was Benedictine practice for the monks to pray *in choro* for the souls of the dead.[16] Whatever the case, it is certain that the adepts upon the isle used toning practices to enhance the vibrational harmonics of the soul transference system. Describing these tones is beyond the scope of this book, but in the *Isle of Avalon* I do describe the measures and ratios of the Mary Chapel – some of which find congruence with the ratios of the natural landscape, for example, the sevenfold geometry of the diamond – and these will be of relevance to those interested.[17]

The observation of celestial events from the Mound and its integration with the geometrical harmonic system suggest this was another place for working with the energies of the Tor. The alignments to winter solstice and the extremes of the lunar cycle perhaps show that the Mound, Tor and springs worked together to accumulate and release energy especially effectively at these times.

Avalon: the Pure Land

In Buddhist tradition, all beings go upon death to the Pure Land of Amitabha. 'Holy beings are sent by Amitabha', I was told by a Lama of a Tibetan lineage, 'to guide the dying or the dead person to the Pure Land where there is peace and plenty of every kind'. The transference of the spirit to the Pure Land, the Lama said, is accomplished in several ways: through practice of the journey during life, through undertaking the journey at the moment of death, and through the loving support of those who understand the nature of the journey. It is especially important not to alarm the spirit of the dead or dying person, but to tell them of the wonderful, peaceful and joyful nature of the Pure Land, and of the kind and loving support provided by the guides sent out to receive them.

It is evident that this practice, or one like it, was performed on the Isle of Avalon in ancient times. Echoes of it are preserved in Celtic texts such as the *Voyage of Bran* that tell of the peace and beauty of 'Emhain', the Otherworld or Avalon, and the freedom from suffering, sickness and death that exists there. The guidance, the Lama explained, was carried out through 'tonal keys that attracted the spirit and gave it access to the crystalline cities below the Tor'. The tones sung and the instruments played in this world resonate with the heavenly music of the Otherworld through the crystalline structures within the Tor. This forms a clear and reassuring pathway for the recently deceased to travel upon.

Upon arrival, the chanting and visualisations of the practitioners in conjunction with the energies of the Tor, allowed 'the pure white essence of the soul to release and ascend the central channel'. The practitioners upon the island were familiar with the journey themselves, so the visualisation of its true and joyful nature could be maintained at all times, and the journeying souls held in peacefulness and love. The Isle of Avalon, the Lama said, was at that time 'a place set apart'. It was 'golden land' devoted to the transition of the soul. It was 'a paradise where perpetual chanting led the souls of the deceased to freedom and fulfilment'.

'In the west', the Buddhic text known as the *Sutra of Amitabha* says, 'there is a world called Utmost Happiness where Amitabha teaches the Dharma. The land is called Utmost Happiness because the inhabitants never suffer, but enjoy every bliss. This land is surrounded by seven tiers of embankments, by seven layers of veiling, and by seven rows of trees ... there are seven pools filled with crystals of every kind, and heavenly music always plays'. The text goes on to describe the other wonders of the Pure Land and its great number of guides and teachers. 'Whoever hears of Amitabha' the text concludes, 'and holds his name with a mind unconfused for one day, two days, three, four, five, six, seven days, then Amitabha and the Assembly of the Holy Ones will appear at the end of life, so that when the end comes the mind will be clear, and the person will be reborn'.

The account of the dowser reminded me of a meeting I had with a Buddhist teacher in 1983. I contacted the teacher, now a Lama, and was sent information that I reproduce in the box above. I could not help but be struck by the similarity between the Buddhist and the Celtic teachings on the Otherworld and the afterlife. Not only is the entrance to the Otherworld located in the west in both traditions, but both describe a sevenfold entranceway, miraculous trees, birds, music and freedom from suffering.

There is no use for keening,
There is nothing harsh or rough,
Only sweet music on the ear
In this familiar well-tilled land.

Without grief, without sorrow,
Without death, without sickness,
These are the signs of Emhain.
Behold! It is no common wonder.

It is beyond compare,
It is a day of lasting weather,
It is a silver land across the sea
On which dragon-stones and crystals fall.[18]

Celtic texts such as the *imrams* (voyages) of Maeldun or Bran, reproduced above, and Buddhist texts like the *Sutra of Amitabha* provide good

indications of the kind of afterlife teaching and assistance that was practised by the initiates of the early school upon the Isle of Avalon. It is
tempting to go further and draw analogies between Gywnn ap Nudd,
Amitabha and other psychopomps (Otherworld guides) in Celtic and
Buddhist tradition. The fairy folk of the Celtic tradition for example
appear in similar ways to the ranks of holy beings in the sutras, and the
subjective nature and the length of time spent in the Otherworld are
the same. But it is sufficient just to draw attention to the matter here
as, no doubt, similarities may also be found with Moslem, Hindu and
other afterlife traditions.

SOUL PORTAL

By 2003, with a good understanding of Otherworld traditions, of soul
transference practices, of energy dynamics and the geology, history and
traditions of the Isle of Avalon, it became essential to bring the material
together and take it further. I needed as it were, a unifying theory of the
soul portal that provided an understanding of the lost Avalonian tradition
of the dead. What exactly was the soul portal on the Tor and how did it
work?

A vital component of the theory presented itself to me when I first
considered the theme of the red and white essences. I went into the topic
of red and white in my previous book, *The Isle of Avalon*. Here I
discussed the alchemical red and white powders of St. Dunstan, the
red and white motifs in the symbols of the Abbey, the red and white
symbols inherent in the British traditions of the Otherworld, the red
and white dragons of Merlin, of Excalibur, of heraldry and so on. I
also described an encounter with 'a fundamental polarity ... experienced
as red and white forces ... that signified the joining of my parent's sperm
and ovum'. But I did not understand how these things related to the soul
portal of Avalon until the Lama I first met in 1983 reminded me of the
teaching on the red and white essences given in the Buddhist tradition.
For example, Sogyal Rinpoche in *The Tibetan Book of Living and Dying*
writes:

> *During the development of the fetus, our father's essence, a nucleus
> that is ... 'white and blissful', rests in the chakra at the crown of
> our head at the top of the central channel. The mother's essence, a
> nucleus that is 'red and hot', rests in the chakra ... located four
> finger-widths below the navel.*

The white and red essences, Rinpoche wrote, are contained within the subtle energy channels of the body and account for the functions of the psychophysical system. At the close of life, the white essence descends the central channel toward the heart inducing an experience of 'whiteness'. The corresponding ascent of the mother's essence induces an experience of 'redness'. When the essences meet in the heart the mind is at last free of thoughts and there dawns what is called the 'Ground Luminousity', or 'the mind of the clear light of death'. 'This consciousness is the innermost subtle mind', added Rinpoche, quoting the Dalai Lama ... 'We call it the Buddha nature, the real source of all consciousness'.[19]

Given the affinity between the water within the body and the water in the body of the earth, I began to glimpse the correspondences between the inner psychophysical processes at the time of death and the outer geophysical aquifer that forms the soul portal within the Tor. I needed to explore how the two systems were related and when I added my study of the energy vortex and of alchemy – especially that of the blood – to the insights of the Lama and Rinpoche, I felt I was on the verge of recreating an understanding of the Otherworld mysteries that was the equivalent in the Western tradition of the long established Pure Land teachings in the East. What follows therefore is an attempt to reconstruct the lost Avalonian Tradition of the Dead.

The upper parts of the human body and the Tor aquifer, the crown of the head and the waters of the White Spring, correspond to an energy vortex of the 'white essence'. The lower parts of the human body and the Tor aquifer, the navel and the waters of the Red Spring, correspond to an energy vortex of the 'red essence'. Through visualization and toning the practitioners of the school upon the Isle of Avalon enhanced the properties of the energy vortices of the mineral-rich water contained within the Tor's two-layer geophysical system, and this corresponded to and supported similar processes in the journey of the soul making the transference to and from the body.

Several practices or means of operation suggested themselves to me:

1. The first is the visualization and the release of the 'red feminine essence' or energy that lies at the base of the system. This rises up the central core of the Tor, while the 'white masculine essence' descends from the crown. From the contribution of physicists and of the psychics who have described the Tor, I recognised the value of visualising these processes as two simultaneous centripetal, contra-rotating vortices coming to a point of stillness at the centre of the core. This is the place of maximum energy, the 'energy canon' of Viktor Schauberger. It is easy to visualise an enormous release of transformational energy at this point, transporting the departing soul swiftly to the other side. The centripetal vortices build up a colossal positive charge that is transformed into a centrifugal negative charge and released in the form of light.

It was difficult for my rational mind to understand exactly how this process worked until I reminded myself of the position taken in the Celtic and Buddhist worldview, by quantum physics and by many contemporary writers like Schauberger and Theodor Schwenk, who refer to the priority of energy. That is, the dynamic interaction of energetic forces develops the natural and external world of form and not the other way around. The soul generates and develops the body; the body does not generate and develop the soul. Energy is *a priori* and the vortex is the form assumed by energy that gives it existence in the physical world.[20]

With this knowledge, it becomes possible to state that the atomic and ionic bonds that form the molecule of water are effectively energy in every part and are influenced at the energetic level in their creation of diverse, complex molecular, crystalline, microbial and cellular forms. By visualising the process of soul transference through the channels and chakras of the body in the correspondingly similar channels, veins and chambers of the Tor, the combination of energies creates a powerful field of harmonic resonance through which the soul is supported and guided on its journey. It is unnecessary to precisely understand how and why the ionic charges of the atoms of iron, hydrogen and oxygen interact and pattern themselves in the way they do. It is only important to know that they can do so in a beneficial and harmonious manner when exposed to positive influences. The Christian monks, the Celtic Druids and the ancient peoples of Avalon knew this – and now it is possible to retrieve and restore this knowledge. (For a first hand account of working with the energy of the Tor see Appendix 1.)

2. The second means of operation differs only slightly. I described earlier how it is easy to visualise a centripetal vortex of energy descending from the sky to a point upon the summit of the Tor to meet another centripetal vortex ascending from the earth. I described the image as a giant egg timer or a descending and ascending dragon. This alternative imagery visualises the red feminine essence rising upwards from the earth like a droplet through the channels of the system at the same time as it visualises the white masculine essence descending from the sky. It then visualises the process of transmutation as they meet within the chamber immediately below the summit of the Tor. I find it easy in this case to see the centrifugal energy vortex focusing upwards rather than outwards. The discarnate soul continues on its journey out through the crown of the Tor in the same manner as it leaves the crown of the head. The task of the operators of the system is to guide the soul directly into the luminosity of the Otherworld.

Through the use of visualisation and especially of toning at the entrances and exits to the system located at the Red and White Springs, the practitioners could adjust the system according to need, and, most considerably, according to the weather! Successive raising of the red 'yin' essence from the root of the system for example, over a period of a week, results in a massive build up of positive charge in the core. This energy builds most effectively in dryer times and, among other things, charges the ions within the system. Effort then directed into encouraging the descent of the solar, stellar and 'yang' essence into the chamber at the top of the core then allows a release of energy – negative ions, most effectively induced by rain and lightning – to aid and assist the journey of the soul to the other side. The system could pulse frequently for a steady process of transference, or pulse intermittently but more strongly for a build up of departing souls in a time of need. I note that tradition says Gwynn ap Nudd gathers up the souls of the deceased at Samhain, 1 November, the beginning of the season when there is most water moving in the caves and passages of the aquifer.

Incidentally, I have no reason to think that the tower currently on the summit of the Tor hinders the working of the system at all. If anything, it enhances it. It is a hollow structure made of natural materials aligned to the main axes of the Tor. It is likely that a circular tower, in resonance with the vortices of energy, would have a greater effect, but as the square tower enhances the vital vertical axis there is no harm done. Moreover, I am of the opinion that the most effective tools for the enhancement of the Tor vortex and transference system are mental, inner practices rather than external constructed forms. The external forms, such as the tower, the energy lines, the geometrical figures, temples, roads and so on, are still functions of mind and only work for or against the system as such. As adjuncts to the inner energy practices, they can enhance them, but they can also confuse the issue. Yes, a sanctuary landscape temple laid out according to ratios in vibrational sympathy to the cosmos, built of elements that focus and enhance the system, is a beneficial tool in the hands of those who understand the *a priori* of energy and intention, but no, it is unnecessary, potentially confusing, and so landscape, however wonderful or however ruined, merely reflects the passing concerns and fashions of the age.

3. The third means of operation has a sexual character and keeps me in mind of the experiential not the abstract nature of the soul transference process. The soul, after all, arrives as a result of sexual activity and the portal of Avalon exists not only for the benefit of outgoing souls but also for incoming souls. It is an entranceway as well as an exit; and so the following practice – with its affinity to contemporary Eastern tantra and the Western alchemical tradition of the 'Royal Marriage' – is more suited to this end.

Over the Tor and the surrounding landscape lies the solar and stellar realm of the white masculine essence or energy vortex. Below this lies the earth, the realm of the red feminine essence or energy vortex. At the Tor, she lifts her hips to present her vulva to the sky. As the cool white essence concentrates through centripetal motion into a nucleus and descends through the summit of the Tor, so the hot red essence rises and meets the white in the central chamber. To aid in the process of conscious and beneficial rebirth, the practitioners upon the island encouraged the souls attracted there along the spirit paths or alignments to incarnate through serene and pleasant awareness of the ecstatic union of the two forces.

The aquifer within the Tor presents a form not unlike a living organism full of thousands of veins, arteries and tiny capillaries through which moves the vital elixir of the universe – water. Beneath the filtering sandstone of the summit the limestone layers fill the water of the topmost spring with calcium. The underlying layers of iron-saturated clays fill the lower spring with iron. The water in one half of the aquifer catalyses its energetic charge in one manner, the other half in another manner. It is possible to conceive of a point midway where the two halves meet or change, where the nature of the electrolytic charges shift and so attract or repel each other. There is a reaction going on within the alchemical retort of the Tor today where the iron and calcium present in the system produce, through the medium of water, a specific bioelectrical charge as their ionic bonds coalesce and dissolve. Through the loose ionic bonds of water, the energy vortices that form the atoms of the minerals in the aquifer are potentised and transformed. This allows them to grow into compound forms, into molecules and crystals of ever-greater complexity and to produce ions with a particularly beneficial energetic charge.[21]

Water: The Supreme Solvent

Science describes the molecule of water as consisting of two hydrogen atoms and one oxygen atom. The hydrogen atom, with a single electron around its central nucleus, is the simplest and most predominant spherical energy vortex – or atomic particle – in the universe, forming over 70% of its atomic mass. The centripetal, inward-turning, simple and loose bonds of the vortex of hydrogen mean that it actively seeks to join with the spherical vortices of other atoms, especially those whose electrons have a complementary ionic charge. The positively charged electron of the hydrogen atom for example seeks to join with the negatively charged electrons of the atom of oxygen to form a water molecule.

The ionic charges in water make it want to hold together, as shown by its capillary action, surface tension and its colloidal, droplet-forming nature. And, at the same time, the simple, loose and fluid energy of the vortex of hydrogen means that it can approach other elements closely and dissolve their ionic bonds. Stimulated by vortical flow forms, the ever-changing ionic nature of water causes the subtle energetic properties of the atoms and molecules of other elements to be dissolved and suspended within it. Vortical flow forms cause water to form ever more energised, complex and adaptive layered structures. Vortices cause water to bring balance to acid or alkaline states, and, when absorbed by those who drink it, vortical flow forms cause water to create and maintain the conditions most conducive for life.

Water is the supreme solvent. The ability of the ionic charge of its atoms to be potentized by the electromagnetic energies of other elements dissolved within it means that water can retain their energy even after being diluted to the point where technically no atoms of the other elements remain. Water can 'hold the memory' of the energy of the substances it has come into contact with no matter how apparently far apart their vortices are. The infinite variety of snowflake and ice crystals demonstrates this ability. No two water crystals are the same as they came into being under unique circumstances of light, temperature, pressure, trace elements, radiation, solar wind, sound, electromagnetic charges and movement upon the hexagonal structural bonding of their constituent atoms.

> **Life is formed by and evolves from the infinite variety of moment-to-moment energetic changes taking place in moving water. Through the sensitive, receptive, coherent yet fluid properties of water, all life is joined together as one.**
>
> As spring water emerges from the ground it carries the properties of the energy of the elements of the body of the earth it has had contact with. Water allows the salts, clays and minerals of the earth and the ionic charges of their atoms to develop through its medium into a 'mature' state. This is demonstrated through the evolving complexity of the molecular and crystalline structures of those elements. At times, this combination and evolution of qualities is extremely beneficial to living cells and organisms. Sometimes the effect is specific and was noted in the past when a spring was said to be excellent for a particular kind of healing. At other times it was known that the efficacy of the water could be enhanced through chanting, stirring, prayer, or a combination of these practices. The practices mimicked the energetic reactions taking place in the tens of thousands of veins of water present in the typical subterranean aquifer and in the vortex formations of water in the air as vapour or upon the earth as liquid.

At auspicious and meteorologically favourable times, the adepts upon the island concentrated upon the central channel within the Tor as the means for supporting the incoming soul to assume form. The red essence at the base of the system – made apparent by the iron emerging in the artesian waters of the Red Spring – and the white essence in the upper part of the system made apparent by the waters of the White Spring, met, and through a selection of practices were enhanced through vibratory fields that sympathetically aided the soul's passage to and from the Otherworld. The meeting of the descending and concentrated droplet of white essence with the ascending droplet of red essence in the resonance chamber at the core of the transference system provided a great opportunity for many souls to exchange matter and energy. The all-important concern of the practitioners was to ensure the transference was one of peacefulness, calm and joy. It was not just a chemical reaction, it was the 'chymical wedding' of the alchemists, and it required the sustained accompaniment of celebratory thoughts and loving intentions. Among the practices employed to achieve the

goal were prayer, visualisation, vibrational toning, dance and sound projection.

The system can work in several ways, but the practices described here follow the same principles. At times when the white and red essences meet and the predominantly centripetal vortices of energy form matter, souls can come in; when the essences part and the vortices release their matter into energy, souls go out. In the past, when the system was better understood and more effectively enhanced, the energy radiating from the core along the alignments drew departing souls to the island and the island at its peak had such a brilliance it could be seen from far away. The predominantly centrifugal vortices dissolving themselves and thus their matter into energy created the luminescence. Einstein's famous formula $E = mc^2$, where c, the constant, the speed of light – or the speed a vortex is required to maintain to create the constancy of form – is multiplied by itself, illustrates the amount of energy released. It is not surprising that people chose not to live in the island at this time given all this psychic, energetic and Otherworldly activity, and the indications are that the school maintained a small number, perhaps only twelve members, at any one time.

Although on the one hand I felt excited that I had begun to understand the nature of the portal upon the Tor, on the other hand I felt in awe of such a thing. It raised many questions. What was to be done with it? Did it still work? What ethical and moral issues were involved? I turned to someone whose tradition still possesses a practice of soul transference – the Lama who told me twenty years ago of the 'crystalline cities' below the Tor – and together we formulated two further practices that those who wish can use to assist in the restoration and functioning of the soul portal of Avalon. One practice follows and the box alongside reproduces the other. Once these intentional practices, or any of the others described here, become familiar to the practitioner, it is important to keep in mind that physical activity enhances them. As described in the exercise, 'The Energy of the Axis Mundi', the practices are complemented by focused physical movement, such as *Tai Chi*, yoga or dance, sound – especially overtone chanting – and breath work.[22]

4. The fourth practice or means of operation focuses upon the release of energy at the time of transference through the soul portal. It is possible to invert the practice to focus upon the convergence of energy at the time of incarnation, but it is sufficient to describe only the release here. Through the understanding of the primary nature of

Meditation: The Crucible of Avalon

Relax in a comfortable position and bring the mind to stillness by contemplating a sublime presence. This presence may be the embodiment of truth, of peace, of goodness or a divine being. It may be a pure radiance, a sound, a fragrance, a vista, or an all-encompassing feeling of love and understanding. See this presence as an infinitely generative source of shining energy over the Isle of Avalon. Know that whatever journey is undertaken, whether being born or dying, all is held in the utmost grace, peace, protection and love by the pure energy of this presence.

Focus attention upon the Tor in the centre of the island. See it in all its beauty. Multiple energies spiral around it and through it. It is alive with energy. It is the portal between the worlds. A deep red pool lies within and at its base, and the radiant presence is in the sky above. There is a wonderful chamber in the heart of the Tor. The chamber may be full of many coloured jewels, a dragon may guard it, it may be full of divine music. . . .

Allow the mind to join with the energy that steadily rises from the red pool of vortex energy at the base of the Tor. Merge with this energy as it slowly concentrates, forms a droplet and rises up the central channel. As it rises, become aware of a pure vortex of energy moving steadily downwards from the presence above. The beautiful and peaceful nature of the sublime radiant presence begins to draw nearer.

As the rising droplet of red energy carries the mind into the chamber at the heart of the Tor so it meets with the indescribable radiant essence of goodness, beauty and truth concentrated into a white droplet descending from above. The two dissolve into each other. Go deeper and deeper into their union.

When thoroughly immersed in this union, in whatever forms, colours or sounds it takes, let a blessing emerge for the soul of all living beings. Let those who are coming into existence at this time, whose consciousness is being drawn to the union of the two essences, be held in the embrace of awareness and truth. See them being held in grace, in the loving and caring hands of many guides and helpers. They are told what is happening to them as they are drawn away from the central chamber to incarnation.

At the same time, let the blessing extend to all whose bodies are failing or have died, and need the guiding radiance from Avalon to

115

draw them home. They come in on every side and are met by the
extended hands of the many helpers and guides. They are clearly
and lovingly told where they are and what is happening to them.
Their sorrow and suffering dissolves away in the blissful union
between the red and the white essences in the crucible of Avalon.
They are urged to seek the pure radiance of the Otherworld. As
they become ready and reassured, see them turn toward the
radiant presence and go on their way. They may go slowly, they
may go swiftly along the lines of energy radiating outward from
the Tor. All that remains of their passing is the radiant presence.

Know that all beings will make this journey one day, so
become familiar with it, and return as often as possible to sustain
and support the passage of the incoming and outgoing souls – be
it for all sentient beings or for one particular being.

---

energy, and especially of the energy vortices that form the being, the
practice shows how the connections with the many elemental qualities
or conditions of this world are withdrawn. The practice proceeds by
acknowledging the elemental qualities that gave substance to the experiences of the life and then releases them. For example, acknowledgement
of what tradition calls the visceral humours takes place and along with
them every particle of matter that shaped, entered and gave energy to
the existence of the body. The acknowledgement, perhaps accompanied
with gratitude, allows the release of the formative elemental particles.
The same can be done for the lungs, the heart and the nervous system,
for air, for water, for fire, for every element – traditionally known as
the ethers – that gave energy, warmth and substance to the existence of
the body. Next, the thoughts and emotions of the life are acknowledged
and in the acknowledgement, the internal energies of the being that gave
rise to those thoughts and feelings, and with them, every accompanying
action, are brought home. The release is undertaken of all that was made,
created, touched, grieved over, enjoyed or lost. Then, every other being,
object, animal, plant, tree, place and so on that gave substance to the life
and gave it shape and form, is acknowledged and in being acknowledged
is released.

As this process develops, the energy centres of the being making the
transference draw in, or take home, the manifestations they created or
were responsible for in life. The vortical energy centres of the being
may be envisaged as chakra centres, or in some other appropriate
energy-body form. There is often a dragon-like quality to these energy

vortex forms. As these energy centres release or withdraw from the elemental qualities they have formed and associated with in life, there is a corresponding increase in their vital or core energy. They become more vigorous around their centripetal points of focus. Sometimes this process is accomplished easily as the energy being willingly and joyfully recognises its true nature, but sometimes there is a reluctance to release the elemental qualities and conditions that gave the soul its physical existence and experiences in life. Obviously it is possible to work through an extremely long list of elemental qualities, other beings, thoughts, feelings, objects and creations that the energy of the transitioning being is responsible for and sometimes this is appropriate (and carried out in obituaries, eulogies, memorial services and so on), but usually it is unnecessary to go into such details. A general yet sustained holding of the atmosphere of acknowledgement and release is sufficient for the process to begin and unfold. The practice given in the box alongside complements this simple process.

The members of the ancient Order of Avalon understood that the system in their hands was concerned not just with the passage of the individual soul but also with the death and rebirth of the human condition. The Tor as *axis mundi*, as the Gateway between the Worlds, allowed access to the cathartic experience of at-one-ment, the times when society undertook death and rebirth as a whole. Here on Avalon, paradise, the Golden Age, was maintained; as however dire the external circumstances, the Tor – in its liminal world among the marshes – offered eternal renewal, restoration and return to the natural order of life. This natural order, described in myth as the Atlantean or the pre-lapsarian age – the time when giants walked the earth and law was maintained through the music of the bard – was established through the connection with the universal forces of life and the elemental powers of creation. The members of the school knew that through the connecting portal of Avalon a collective experience of release and coalescence could take place. Their work consisted of holding an energy field that vibrated in sympathy with the energies of creation. This process – described as the establishment of paradise, as the building of the heavenly city, 'the New Jerusalem' on earth – laid the basis for a world order built upon the harmonies and ratios of the cosmos. It was and it still is this belief that gives Avalon its traditions: that it is the New Jerusalem, that a great temple dedicated to spirit is here, that the greatest spiritual teachers came here, that King Arthur and the Holy Grail are buried here, and that it will be a force forever in the unfoldment of things to come.

ENDNOTES

1. Ash and Hewitt, 1990, pp. 24–31.

2. C. Coates, 1996.

3. Ash and Hewitt, op. cit.

4. M. Emoto, 1999.

5. J. Foster Forbes, 1945, *Giants, Myths and Megaliths*.

6. Olive Pixley, 1939, *Psychometry,* unpublished, courtesy of Gun Pelham.

7. The research into these alignments was carried out by observation on the ground, by study of recorded material and by computer supported testing of the mathematical and astronomical data. I am indebted to Sig Lonegren for checking and providing detail of the archaeoastronomy.

8. The events of the 2006 major standstill are 4 April for the most northerly, and 29 September for the most southerly, although other events in that year also fall close to the extremes.

9. For more on the diamond see N. Mann, 2001, pp. 77–81.

10. A. Thom in M. Williams, *Glastonbury: A Study in Patterns*, RILKO, 1969. Thom's major work, *Megalithic Sites in Britain*, Oxford, 1967, shows the interest of the prehistoric astronomer in alignments where the sun or moon roll up or down hillsides on the significant dates described here. The map reference Thom provides is ST 510390.

11. A. Thom, op cit. The point being that observers upon the Isle of Avalon in the early Bronze Age could use the Black Mountain in Wales (ST 822225) to refine the declination of the northernmost setting point of the moon. Marke Pawson drew this to my attention. Marke also thought that although the Black Mountain is on the correct alignment, the peaks that form the most distant points visible from the Tor are in fact Sugarloaf, just beyond Crickhowel, and Skirrid Fawr and Borenge, south and north of Abergavenny respectively.

12. Jane Roberts, 'Somerset Legendary Geomancy' in Roberts, 1978, pp. 64–70.

13. In an account of work in progress in 2002, archaeologist N. Hollindrake suggested the existence of the temple on the basis of a circular foundation upon the summit of the Tor. The evidence is slight. Geoffrey Ashe thought the temple might never have got beyond the foundations.

14. The Lake Villages are the prime evidence in Britain of the Celtic 4th century BCE culture concurrent with the eponymous site of La Tène on the Swiss lakes. Excavated by Arthur Bulleid in the 19th century, the absence of burial places for the Lake Villages gave rise to much speculation by him and others as to where they should be. See for example P. Rahtz, 1993, pp. 22–23.

15. For accounts of NDE's and otherworldly experiences see Serena Roney-Dougal, 2003, Ash and Hewitt, 1990, pp. 149–168 and R. Moody, *Life after Life*, Bantam 1976.

16. For more on perpetual choirs see J. Michell, 1990, and F. Bligh Bond, 1918. For the underground tunnels of Glastonbury see Ann Pennick in A. Roberts, 1978, and J. Morland, 1870, *Underground Glastonbury*, in Glastonbury Antiquarian Society Publication Vol. 1.

17. N. Mann, 2001, pp. 99–109. The synthesis of twelve-fold and seven-fold systems is especially remarkable, but other patterns based upon the geometry of the Abbey are also prominent. See also J. Michell, 1983, ch 6 and Tom Kenyon, *Sound Transformations*, (CD) 2000.

18. From *Imram Brain maic Febail*, 'The Voyage of Bran son of Febail'. The version I give here relies upon the translations of Kuno Meyer, 1895, and Lady Gregory, 1904. For the *Sutra of Amitabha* refer to the Buddhist Text Translation Society.

19. Sogyal Rinpoche, 1993, pp. 248–254.

20. Ash and Hewitt, 1990, p. 26.

21. See C. Coates, 1996, T. Schwenk, 1989, and Charlie Ryrie, 1998, *The Healing Energies of Water*, Gaia Books, London.

22. For an understanding of the tonal sounds involved in these processes I highly recommend the work of Tom Kenyon. For example, *Sound Transformations*, 2000, or visit www.tomkenyon.com.

APPENDICES

APPENDIX 1. A HEALING ACCOUNT

'After living at the White Spring for a number of years', wrote Ella Portman, 'I learnt that the water that runs through the labyrinth under the Tor is energised by it like an accumulator. The spring emerges in a natural chamber deep in the ground behind the reservoir. It is a gentle but extremely powerful energy. I call it the White Lady, because although its energy is formed by the dance of male and female energies, the presence of a white lady always came to me whenever I connected with it.

'As the years went by, I progressively learnt how to open up to the challenges of the White Spring. It became apparent how damaged the spring is. It seems to be a place where the veil between the worlds is thin. It is thus a connecting place and also a passing over place where souls can move in and out. It was in this environment that I learnt about soul rescue.

'In my healing work, people often had what appeared to be past life memories of the White Spring as a place of power, the power of both creation and destruction. They remembered being wounded by the misuse of this power. It seems as if this energy was misappropriated repeatedly in the past. The wounds went deep, and all seemed to point toward the need for healing the wounded inner feminine spirit and the healing of the separation between male and female energies.

'During my years there, I felt the damage done to the energy of the spring as it was misused. A backlog, a traffic jam of lost and bewildered souls would build up, held by the disturbed energy of the place. Sometimes their disturbed presence was so strong it made our musical instruments play themselves or the bedsprings hum! The water would also wail like souls crying for release. Eventually I learnt to simply listen and ask them what they needed. Then by asking for help from the spirit Guardians of the spring, I learnt how the distressed souls could move on. I was shown how to do this in my dreams as I slept over the spring.

'When the energy field is clear the feeling is very beautiful, very peaceful. Yet because the magnetic and electrical energies are so strong, the creative force so great, people are attracted to the place to try to control the power. The building of the reservoir was an attempt to control the power. The exorcism of the fairies from the Tor by St. Collen with his phial of holy water was an attempt to control it. The forcing of water through pipes is an attempt to control it. These are attempts by those who think they know the truth to impose their will upon a natural and beautiful system for their own ends. The combined effects of all the misuse and control has resulted in a much damaged energy system, with a great entangled mishmash of earth, water and electrical energies, where nothing flows as it needs to anymore. This is the state of the spring today.

'It feels to me that the system is restored by deeply tuning in to the energy of spring with humility. I certainly learnt to never to do anything without connecting with the guardians of the spring: the White Lady essence and the elementals of the earth. I learnt that the old pattern of misuse and abuse is just repeated again and again when I thought I knew what needed to happen and imposed my own ideas. I also learnt that the positive energy field is enhanced through the loving union of male and female energies. The opposite is created when there is fear or controlling behaviour between men and women. The energy of the place acts as an amplifier – when there is disturbance in the water it is felt intensely by the soul, when there is peace in the soul the harmony in the system is blissful. When I am in tune, aware and centred simply in my inner presence the loving harmonious energy that flows stabilises the whole energy field and the psychic disturbances settle'.

APPENDIX 2. ABDUCTION ACCOUNTS

The first abduction account is of Melwas, King of the Summerland, who took Queen Guinevere to his Tor-top stronghold. King Arthur came to rescue her and the Abbot of Glastonbury effected mediation.[1] This medieval story is prefigured by a second, older account told in the *Mabinogion*, where Gwynn ap Nudd abducts Creiddylad from Gwythyr. Gwynn is besieged in his stronghold until mediation is effected, in this case, by Arthur.[2] It is hard to know what these legends mean. As both Guinevere and Creiddylad have solar associations and because both Melwas and Gwynn ap Nudd are guides to the dead, what seems to be described here is a transition from the dark to the light half of the year and back again. The solar goddess goes back and forth between the worlds in the manner of Persephone.

The third account, from an anonymous source, describes abductions not by humans but by beings from other worlds. It may throw light upon the early accounts given above. 'Water', the source said, 'is the medium of life throughout the universe. The simple, ubiquitous and fluid hydrogen atom allows life to emerge wherever there is the opportunity. Where there is water – atoms of hydrogen and oxygen moving in heliacal spirals – molecular complexity develops. This leads to the evolution of microbial and genetic life forms.

'Evolution takes place through the influence of energy fields upon water that holds elements of every kind in its solution. Some of these influences come from the earth, some from the sun and moon. In the right circumstances, the elements dissolving and coalescing in water and so altering their energetic bonds, can respond to subtle influences from extremely distant sources, even those beyond the solar system, as far away as the galactic core. The goal of these distant sources is genetic evolution. Water-evolved life forms across the universe – some of which are far more complex than ours on earth – are actively seeking to promote life elsewhere. Some of these life forms however are doing this from the desire to support only that which supports themselves. Their interest is self-motivated and not necessarily for the well being of sentient life on individual planets like our earth. Their genes, in effect, are in need of infusions from healthy, young and resilient life forms. The Tor has attracted the interest of those seeking such genetic infusions, as it is a double vortex of water based energy with the power to influence the genetic transactions of life incarnating on earth.

'At times it is possible for the self-interested life forms to feed off the vortex and abduct genetic information, but mostly this is impossible due to the counterforce of collective beneficial intention. The presence of beings that would appear as angels if we could see them – healing, protecting and medicinal presences, with huge multi-faceted force fields, holding the power of love – protect us. It is possible to work with these beings; but it is also necessary to understand that our

123

perception of them is severely distorted from this dimension. Their presence is only visible to us in the universal energy dynamic encoded in the genes. Here, collectively focused beneficial intention, whether in prayer, meditation or simply intelligent goodwill, supports and sustains their efforts. This prevents the usurpation of the system, not so much by those with 'evil' intention – as it is 'good' intention from their perspective – but from any purpose other than the universal good'.

APPENDIX 3. DRAGONS

Dragons are alluded to in several places in this book and it is helpful to briefly describe them here. A dragon is the name given to a multi-dimensional being that exists, transforms and moves in vortex formations. Dragons are the energy 'behind' forms in much the same manner as the Devas described for example, by W. Tudor Pole, Dorothy Maclean and by other writers from Findhorn.[3] Dragons are at once visible and invisible through their ability to be present in the elements yet command the energy vortices that form those elements. They can 'shed their skin' to move through the many dimensions of the universe, the limits of which for us are determined by the speed of light. Dragons are therefore masters of the time, space and matter continuum. They are capricious, humorous, benign, malevolent and indifferent. They can be seen with the non-localised vision of the soul, but they will not willingly admit to it, preferring to remain in mime. Magicians have learnt to recognise and command them, but as dragons prefer to command themselves the practice is inadvisable. However, gardeners, foresters, acupuncturists, hydrologists and sailors, for example, work with them all the time. Animals are also acutely aware of their presence and will adjust their actions accordingly. Observation of the in-turning and out-turning nodes in air, fire and, best of all, in moving water, provide excellent reference points for deeper meditation on the nature of dragons. Acquiring an understanding of the nature of dragons is extremely useful in developing the practices necessary for the enhancement of energy vortices.

ENDNOTES

1. Caradoc of Llancarfan, *Vita Gildae*.
2. *The Mabinogion*, trans. J. Gantz, 1976, pp. 148, 159 and 168.
3. For example, *The Findhorn Garden*, 1976.

BIBLIOGRAPHY

Armitage Robinson, J. 1926, *Two Glastonbury Legends: King Arthur and St Joseph of Arimathea*, Cambridge University Press.

Ash, David & Hewitt, Peter, 1990, *Science of the Gods*, Gateway Books, Bath.

Ashe, Geoffrey: (1) 1968 (editor), *The Quest for Arthur's Britain*, Paladin. (2) 1979, *The Glastonbury Tor Maze*, Gothic Image. (3) 1982, *Avalonian Quest*, London.

Benham, Patrick 1993, *The Avalonians*, Glastonbury, Gothic Image.

Bligh Bond, Frederick (1) 1909, *The Architectural Handbook of Glastonbury Abbey*, Glastonbury. (2) 1918, *The Gate of Remembrance,* Oxford.

Bullied, Arthur 1958, *The Lake Villages of Somerset*, (5th edition), Glastonbury.

Caradoc of Llancarfan, 'Vita Gildae' in *Gildas: The Ruin of Britain,* ed. Williams, Hugh, Cymmrodorion Record Series, No. 3, Pt. 2, London, 1901. Also contains 'De Excidio et Conquestu Britanniae' by Gildas.

Carley, James P. (1) 1981, 'Melkin the Bard and Esoteric Tradition at Glastonbury Abbey', in *The Downside Review*, 99. (2) 1988, *Glastonbury Abbey*.

Coates, Callum 1996, *Living Energies: An Exposition of Concepts Related to the Theories of Viktor Schauberger,* Gateway Books, Bath.

Coles, J. & Orme, B. (1) 1982, *Prehistory of the Somerset Levels.* Somerset Levels Project. (2) 1986, *Sweet Track to Glastonbury: The Somerset Levels in Prehistory*, London.

Eliade, Mircea 1958, *Patterns in Comparative Religion*, Sheed & Ward.

125

Emoto, Masaru 1999, *The Message from Water*, HADO Kyoikusha, Tokyo.

Fortune, Dion 1934, *Avalon of the Heart*, Aquarian Press 1971.

Gennaro, Gino 1979, *The Phenomena of Avalon: The First Heliocentric Book for Two Thousand Years*, Cronos Publications.

Geoffrey of Monmouth, *The History of the Kings of Britain*, Trans., Thorpe, L., Penguin, 1966.

Gildas, see 'Life of Gildas' and 'Life of St Collen' in Baring-Gould, S. & Fisher, J., *Lives of the British Saints*, 1911. (See also Caradoc of Llancarfan.)

Giraldus Cambrensis, *The Historical Works*, trans., Wright, T., Bohn, G., 1863.

Hardy, Peter 1999, *The Geology of Somerset*, Ex Libris Press, Bradford on Avon.

Hearne, Thomas 1722, *The History and Antiquities of Glastonbury*.

John of Glastonbury, *Chronicle*, trans., Carley, B., Boydell 1985.

Jones, Kathy, 2000, *In the Nature of Avalon*, Ariadne Publications, Glastonbury.

Leach, Peter 2001, *Roman Somerset*, The Dovecote Press, Wimborne.

The Mabinogion, trans. Gantz, J., Penguin, 1976.

Maltwood, Katherine 1929, *A Guide to Glastonbury's Temple of the Stars*, London.

Mann, Nicholas, (1) 1985, *The Cauldron and the Grail*, Glastonbury. (2) 1986 and 1993, *Glastonbury Tor*, Glastonbury. (3) 2001, *The Isle of Avalon*, Green Magic, London.

Marrin, West, 2002, *Universal Water: The Ancient Wisdom and Scientific Theory of Water*, Inner Ocean, Maui.

Matthews, Benjamin, 1751, *The Virtues and Efficacy of the Water of Glastonbury*, London, (Somerset Studies Library, Taunton).

Michell, John (1) 1983, *The New View Over Atlantis*, Thames & Hudson. (2) 1988, *The Dimensions of Paradise*, Thames & Hudson. (3) 1990, *New Light on the Ancient Mysteries of Glastonbury*, Gothic Image Publications, Glastonbury.

Rahtz, Philip (1) 1964, *Excavations at Chalice Well, Glastonbury*, P.S.A.N.H.S. Vol. 108, pp145–163. (2) 1974, Rahtz and S. Hirst, *Beckery Chapel, Glastonbury, 1967–68*, (Archaeological Report), Glastonbury. (3) 1971, *Excavations on Glastonbury Tor, Somerset, 1964–6*, R.A.I. (4) 1993, *Glastonbury*, English Heritage, London.

Richardson, L. 1928, *Wells and Springs of Somerset*, Geological Survey, London.

Roberts, Anthony 1978, *Glastonbury: Ancient Avalon, New Jerusalem*, Rider.

Roney-Dougal, Serena 2003, *The Fairy Faith*, Green Magic, London.

Saward, Jeff 1984, *Caerdroia* 14.

Schwenk, Theodor (1) 1965, *Sensitive Chaos: The Creation of Flowing Forms in Water and Air*, Steiner Press, London. (2) 1989, *Water: The Element of Life*, Anthropomorphic Press, Hudson NY.

Sogyal, Rinpoche 1993, *The Tibetan Book of Living and Dying*, Harper Collins.

Tudor Pole, Wellesley, (1) 1965, *A Man Seen Afar*, Neville Spearman. (2) 1968, *Writing on the Ground*, Neville Spearman.

Walsh, Terry 1993, *Global Sacred Alignments*, University of Avalon Press, Glastonbury.

Warner, Rev. Richard 1826, *An History of the Abbey of Glaston*, Bath.

Welch F. B. A. and Crookall R. 1935, *British Regional Geology: Bristol and Gloucester District*, D.S.I.R., London.

William of Malmesbury, 'De Antiquitate Glastoniensis Ecclesiae', in Scott, J., *The Early History of Glastonbury*, Boydell, Woodbridge, 1981. Or, *The Antiquities of Glastonbury*, trans. Frank Lomas, Facsimile reprint 1992, J.M.F. Book, Llanerch.

Wright, George W. (1) 1870, *The Chalice Well, or Blood Spring, and its Traditions*, Glastonbury Antiquarian Society Publication 1. (2) 1894, 'The History of Glastonbury During the Last Forty Years' in *Bulleids of Glastonbury*, Armynell Goodall, Taunton, 1984.

INDEX

Green Magic Publishing

Green Magic Publishing is an independent publishing house based in the South West of England.

We hope you enjoyed reading *Energy Secrets of Glastonbury Tor* by Nicholas Mann – our other titles are:

Advanced Wiccan Spirituality by Kevin Saunders (ISBN 095429632x)
Book of Shadows Large (ISBN 0954296389), Small (ISBN 0954296303)
The Faery Faith by Serena Roney-Dougal (ISBN 0953663175)
Wiccan Spirituality by Kevin Saunders (ISBN 0953663167)
Teenage Witch's Book of Shadows by Anna de Benzelle & Mary Neasham (ISBN 0953663159)
Underworld of the East by James S Lee (ISBN 0953663116)

Our new titles for 2004 include -

Spirit of the Green Man by Mary Neasham (ISBN 0954296370)
Green Spirituality by Rosa Romani (ISBN 0954296362)

All Green Magic books are available from your local bookshop.

Green Magic is always interested in receiving manuscripts, especially in the fields of Magic and Wicca, Sacred Landscape and Spirituality.

Green Magic Publishing
The Long Barn
Sutton Mallet
Somerset   TA7 9AR
TEL/FAX 01278 722888
www.greenmagicpublishing.com
email: info@greenmagicpublishing.com

The Isle of Avalon
SACRED MYSTERIES OF ARTHUR AND GLASTONBURY

Nicholas R. Mann

Avalon, a site of great power, revered since ancient times as an entrance to, and exit from, the Otherworld. *Isle of Avalon* illustrates and describes the physical and sacred topography of the Isle as well as its symbols, architecture and history. It gives detailed explanations about the Tor, the Glastonbury Zodiac, the Abbey, the Tor labyrinth, the St Michael leyline and much more.

This is an updated and revised edition of the first book to provide a coherent context in which to understand Avalon's many mysteries.

"*Nicholas Mann explores Avalon in impressive detail.*" **Geoffrey Ashe.**

"*Everything you wanted to know about the sacred mysteries of Glastonbury.*" **Third Stone.**

"*Mann provides an impressive overview of Glastonbury's history and mythology. An enjoyable and valuable read*" **Fortean Times.**

Nicholas R. Mann is the author of many books, most recently *Energy Secrets of Glastonbury Tor* (Green Magic 2004). Other titles include *Reclaiming the Gods* (Green Magic 2002) and *Druid Magic* (Llewellyn 2000). He lives in Glastonbury, England.

The Isle of Avalon by Nicholas R. Mann.
King Arthur / Celtic Wisdom / Sacred Landscape.
Price £9.99 / $16.99   ISBN 0953663132   Illustrated.

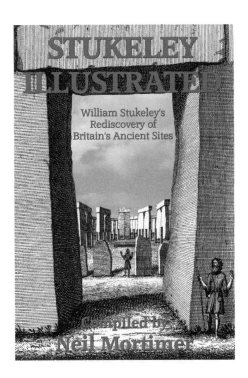

STUKELEY ILLUSTRATED

William Stukeley's Rediscovery of Britain's Ancient Sites

Compiled by Neil Mortimer

William Stukeley was the first man to chronicle the greatest prehistoric stone circles in the world, Stonehenge and Avebury.

One of the eighteenth century's most remarkable characters, he was friend and colleague to some of the most gifted men of his time, including Sir Isaac Newton.

Stukeley's work laid the foundations for the modern study of prehistoric monuments, influenced the Druidic revival and inspired some of William Blake's most celebrated paintings.

For the first time *Stukeley Illustrated* brings together over 100 of the best engravings from his most brilliant books. It shows how this meticulous and inspired draughtsman changed the way we look at ancient sites. It is a tribute to an increasingly relevant figure, and is indispensable to anyone interested in the sacred sites and landscapes of the British Isles.

"A fine tribute to a great man" - **John Michell** (Author of *View Over Atlantis*)

"Highly recommended" - **Avalon**

Stukeley Illustrated Compiled by Neil Mortimer
Biography / Archaeology / Sacred Landscape.
Price £9.99 / $16.99 ISBN 0954296338 Illustrated.

Reclaiming The Gods
Magic, Sex, Death and Football

Nicholas R. Mann

In the same way as the Goddess has been reclaimed in recent years, this book reclaims the God. Nicholas Mann in this vibrant work shows how the figure of the God has become monopolised, marginalised and corrupted, to our great loss.

The restoration of the God in our lives will liberate our individual spiritual experience, enabling us to see with new insight the reality of good and evil. To understand the true nature of our sexual passions, our relationship to others and the world in all its true beauty.

Here we revisit the Trickster, the Hunter, the Shape-Shifter, the Protector, Craftsman, Lover - the Gods of Wisdom, Fertility, Wealth and Laughter that still resonate in our lives today.

"A valuable and original work by a popular writer of contemporary spirituality" - **Avalon**

"Offers an intriguing and useful resource for the male psyche" - **Sacred Hoop**

"This could become one of the classics" - **Pagan Dawn**

Reclaiming the Gods by Nicholas R. Mann
Mythology / Spirituality / Sexuality
Price £9.99 / $16.99   ISBN 0953663183

Handfasting
A Practical Guide

Mary Neasham

This is the first book published in the UK about handfasting! It will take you on a historical journey, starting with pre-Christian times. It describes the customs and traditions associated with betrothal from times and places in the world where our forbears were in tune with the changing seasons and the natural rhythms of the world they lived in.

The increasing popularity of handfasting is recognition that the current alternatives of church or civil ceremonies offer little in the way of deeper meaning in our increasingly pagan times.

In this book, Mary Neasham offers practical advice on creating your own handfasting ceremony. A very modern way to commit to another person based on the lore and customs of our ancestors.

"A treasury of information, useful and wise" - **Glennie Kindred** (Author of *Sacred Celebrations*)

"An excellent book written to suit the initiated, the curious and the layperson. Highly recommended" - **Avalon**

"A very accessible, yet comprehensive guide" - **Pentacle**

Handfasting by Mary Neasham
Marriage / Spirituality / Customs
Price £9.99 / $16.99 ISBN 0954296311

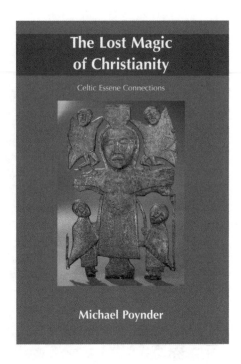

Lost Magic of Christianity is a startlingly original study of the Ancient Wisdom Tradition and Celtic Christianity in Ireland and the West. It unlocks the secrets of Stone and Bronze Age metaphysics that influenced the Gnostic practices of the early priesthood. These priests were vibrant seers, healers and highly skilled astromathematicians, expressing the oneness between human beings, nature and the living spirit of the Christ principle.

However this pagan Christianity magic was soon to be eroded and destroyed by the patriarchal dogma of a debased male priesthood. Our inner mythology and folk memory were taken from us in order to control us.

Lost Magic of Christianity offers enlightened explanations as we begin to shed religion and take responsibility for our divine self in the new millennium.

"An innovative and unusual study of the Ancient Wisdom Tradition. A unique book" - **Celtic Connections**

"Seriously thought provoking reading" - **Pagan Dawn**

"Poynder's fresh look at our ancient heritage suggests a few more pieces of the puzzle that we can put in place" - **Nexus**

The Lost Magic Of Christianity by Michael Poynder
New Age / Spirituality / Ancient Mysteries
Price £9.99 / $16.99 ISBN 0953663108   Ilustrated